IN THE
FOOTSTEPS OF
KINGS

A GUIDE TO WALKS IN AND AROUND
KILMARTIN GLEN

SHARON WEBB

WITH CONTRIBUTIONS BY
SANDRA BARDWELL AND RODDY REGAN

PHOTOGRAPHY BY AARON WATSON

First published in 2012
Reprinted 2013, 2015

Kilmartin Museum Trust
Kilmartin
Argyll
PA31 8RQ
Scotland

Registered Charity SC022744

Tel: 01546 510278

www.kilmartin.org

Maps have been reproduced by permission of Ordnance Survey
on behalf of HMSO. © Crown copyright 2012. All rights reserved.
Licence number 100052523.

ISBN: 978-0-9533674-6-7

A CIP catalogue record for this book is available from the
British Library.

Designed by Aaron Watson.

Printed and bound in the UK.

CONTENTS

FOREWORD

I was very pleased to be asked to write the Foreword for Kilmartin Museum's new Walking Guide as I have long been a supporter of the work of the Museum. For over fifteen years they have been instrumental in protecting and promoting the very rich archaeological landscape of the areas covered by the walks. Kilmartin Glen, Kilmichael Glen, Knapdale and Craignish are packed full of exciting finds. This book, and every one of the walks included, will give you a flavour of why this part of Argyll has been so important in shaping Scotland's past.

The walks chosen also reflect the incredible beauty of the landscape – they will take you from the Celtic rainforests at Crinan Wood and Taynish, across the ancient peat bog of Mòine Mhór, along the cliff tops abutting the spectacular Sound of Jura at Castle Dounie, and to the majestic beach of Kilmory Bay. Here are some of the last truly unspoiled places in Britain – but at all of them we can find evidence of how our ancestors lived, worked and died amongst this at times hard, but always beautiful, landscape.

There is a walk for everyone. For those with restricted mobility, for those who cannot go out without man (or woman's) 'best friend', for those with only an hour to spare – there is a walk for you. There are also some longer, more challenging walks, where the only thing you are likely to see is an otter, red squirrel or beaver! I am looking forward to trying all of them – I hope you enjoy them too and may the weather be with you!

Mick Aston

Professor Mick Aston

Honorary Professor at Bristol, Durham and Exeter Universities and former Archaeological Consultant and Director to Time Team

Ballymeanoch Standing Stones (walk 6)

The Project Team

Sandra Bardwell (walks testing and walks text), Anne Smart (editing, proof reading, ground checking walks), Ailsa Raeburn (fund raising, project management, image research), Roddy Regan (maps, editing, historical research), Dr Aaron Watson (design, photography) and Dr Sharon Webb (project management, introductory guide to the archaeology, monument descriptions, ground checking walks).

Acknowledgements

We would like to thank Reverend Clifford Acklam, Jane Allan, Dr Annette Anderton, Dr Roger Anderton, Gilbert and Jean Black, Gordon Brechin, Dr Ewan Campbell (University of Glasgow), Malcolm Campbell, Trevor Cowie, Steven Farr (Historic Scotland, HS), Colin Ferguson, Gordon Gray Stephens, John Halliday (Scottish Natural Heritage, SNH), Robert Hay, Alex Howie (British Waterways), Lynn Jones, Tim and Margaret Lister, Sue MacLean, the McNair family, Iain Malcolm, Christopher Marshall, Alan Mitchell (Scottish Woodlands Trust), Mike Murray, Rosemary Neagle, Stuart Needham, Nick Purdy (Forestry Commission Scotland, FCS), Kit Read (HS), Matt Ritchie (FCS), Dr John Raven (HS), Dr Alan Saville (National Museums Scotland, NMS), Dr Alison Sheridan (NMS), Laura Skelton, David Smart, Ros Walker, Helen Watt (FCS), Sally Wilkin, and Caroline Younger, for ground checking walks, making helpful comments on the text and for providing information.

Assistance with proofreading the text was freely given by

Sheila Clark and Jane Allan, for which we thank them.

Grateful appreciation is due to Dr Alison Sheridan (NMS) for allowing us access to as yet unpublished material on the prehistory of Kilmartin Glen, and to Dr Katherine Forsyth (University of Glasgow) for sharing her new reading of the Ogham at Dunadd with us. We would also like to thank Gilbert Márcus for assistance with Gaelic and Norse place names.

Special thanks are due to Robin Malcolm for giving very useful advice and information on the history of the Poltalloch Estate and the Malcolm family.

We would like to thank Hugh Andrew, Doreen Grove and Georgina Hobhouse for providing advice on how to create this book.

A number of the images have been provided by other organisations and we would like to express our gratitude to Betty Common at SNH, The Royal Commission on the Ancient and Historical Monuments of Scotland, The National Museum of Scotland, Culture and Sport Glasgow (Museums), Karl Mercer and the Kirnan Estate. All other images are copyright Aaron Watson/Kilmartin Museum.

Sharon Webb would like to give a special thanks to Anne Smart and Ailsa Raeburn for their persistence and patience during the production of this book and to Professor Mick Aston for writing the Foreword.

Finally, we are very grateful to the following organisations for generously providing funding for this book: Museums Galleries Scotland, Historic Scotland, and Forestry Commission Scotland.

The view from Barr Mór trail (walk 22)

Introduction

The first section in this book contains a brief overview of the natural, social, political and cultural events that have shaped the landscape of Mid Argyll and its people over the last 13,000 or so years. Prehistoric dates are given as 'BC' dates, and we have continued the long tradition of describing periods in prehistory as Mesolithic, Neolithic, Chalcolithic, Bronze and Iron ages. This system – more than a century old now – is fraught with problems, but is nonetheless still useful as a general system, and is perhaps more easily understood than describing events in millennia.

Kilmartin Museum concentrates on the prehistoric and early historic periods and so the archaeological and historical overview focuses on this period rather than on the later historical era. We fully acknowledge that the summary of the later centuries is a somewhat breathless rush through Scottish history! However, we have chosen to focus on earlier periods because most of the monuments you will see on your walks date to this time. Later historical events in Argyll have been well documented elsewhere and there is simply not the space in this volume to expand and analyse the many interesting issues and problems that more modern times raise, but we hope that it will spark an interest. To help you find out more, there are suggestions for further reading on the later periods of history at the end of this book.

Many of the ideas, thoughts and theories expressed here have already been set down on paper by archaeologists and historians, but for ease of

---

Prehistoric Timeline – Scotland

Upper Palaeolithic activity: c11000 BC (c13,000 years ago)

Mesolithic: c9800 BC to c4500/4000 BC (c11,800 to c6,500/6,000 y.a.)

Early Neolithic: c4000 BC to c3500 BC (c6,000 to c5,500 y.a.)

Middle Neolithic: c3500 BC to c3000 BC (c5,500 to c5,000 y.a.)

Late Neolithic: c3000 BC to c2500 BC (c5,000 to c4,500 y.a.)

Chalcolithic (Copper Age): c2500 BC to c2200 BC (c4,500 to c4,200 y.a.)

The Early Bronze Age: c2200 BC to c1600 BC (c4,200 to c3,600 y.a.)

Middle and Later Bronze Age: c1600 BC to c800 BC (c3,600 to c2,800 y.a.)

Iron Age and Early Historic Period: c800 BC to c1000 AD (c2,800 to c1000 y.a.)

reading, references have been kept out of the main body of the introductory text. The most influential works appear in the further reading section, and you can obtain a full bibliography from our website www.kilmartin.org.

The second part of the book contains information on 25 walks, through which you can explore the most important and impressive archaeological monuments and areas of natural heritage in Kilmartin Glen, Kilmichael Glen, North Knapdale and Craignish.

How to Responsibly Enjoy this Working Landscape and the Scottish Outdoor Access Code

We want you to enjoy this place, but please remember that it is a working landscape. Respect all signs and notices you see and adhere to the Scottish Outdoor Access Code which asks that you 'Enjoy Scotland's Outdoors Responsibly'. The key aspects of the code are to:

- Take responsibility for your own actions
- Respect the interests of other people
- Care for the environment

You can pick up a copy of the full code at Kilmartin Museum, at the Scottish Natural Heritage Office at Kilmory Industrial Estate, Lochgilphead or find it online at www.outdooraccess-scotland.com

Please stick to designated paths to avoid causing erosion at ancient sites. Do not light fires near or on ancient monuments as fire can damage the site. Do not remove moss or grass from prehistoric sites, especially rock art sites. Although it is tempting to see if you can make your own discovery, you could end up causing irreparable damage to a site.

We want future generations to be able to enjoy this amazing landscape, just as you are doing today.

Dogs are welcome on some routes, but must be kept under control at all times. Some walks request dogs to be under close control – by this we mean they must be kept on a short lead. In the spring, loose dogs may disturb ground nesting birds. Never take your dogs into fields where there are notices asking you not to, or into fields with young stock. Please clear up after your dog because people and livestock may be put at risk.

When walking on ground owned by Forestry Commission Scotland, please be aware that these are places to work in as well as enjoy. Watch out for vehicles and follow any signs you see to ensure you have a safe visit.

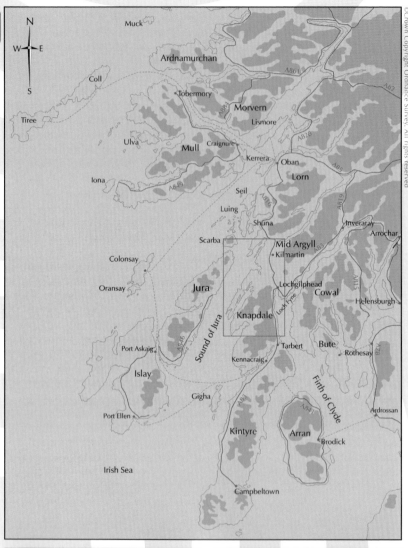

N
W   E
S

Muck
Ardnamurchan
A861
A82
Coll
Tobermory
Morvern
Tiree
Lismore
Ulva
Mull
Craignure
A828
Iona
A849
Kerrera
Oban
Lorn
A85
Seil
Luing
A816
Shuna
A819
Scarba
Mid Argyll
Inveraray
Arrochar
Kilmartin
Colonsay
Jura
Lochgilphead
Cowal
A815
Oransay
Loch Fyne
Helensburgh
Knapdale
Port Askaig
Sound of Jura
A546
Tarbert
Bute
Rothesay
Kennacraig
A83
Islay
Firth of Clyde
Gigha
A841
Ardrossan
Port Ellen
Kintyre
Arran
Brodick
Irish Sea
Campbeltown

How to Use this Guide

At the start of the 'Walks Section' there is a main map showing all 25 walks contained in this guide. Each walk is numbered and contains a local map, summary information, a description of the walk and information about points of archaeological or natural heritage interest.

Mid Argyll is covered by Sheets 55, 56 and 62 of the 1:50,000 Landranger Series Ordnance Survey Maps. This guide has been designed to be used in conjunction with the OS maps; however, not all walks are shown as footpaths on the OS map so the maps given in this book are detailed enough to be used on their own.

The map for a given route will show monuments on the walk as a red dot. You will also see monuments indicated by a yellow dot, which you may walk past, or which are close to your route, but it is not practical, or necessarily advisable, to visit them.

The particular route which you will be following is marked by a red dotted line. Other walks which link to your route are indicated by a green line if they are in this book, or by a blue line if they are not.

Some of the walks included here were created or upgraded by the Dalriada Project[1], a Lottery Funded Landscape Partnership Scheme which aimed to make the most of the area's cultural and natural heritage. There are, of course, many more walks in Mid Argyll. You can find out more about these and what else there is to do in the area, as well as see some of the artefacts that have been found here, by visiting Kilmartin Museum.

Kilmartin Glen

The nation we now call Scotland has been shaped by many forces, geological, natural, cultural – it is a land steeped in history, and this is very apparent in Kilmartin Glen. Today this beautiful Glen is far removed from the political centre of Scotland, but this was not always so. In the 1980s the Royal Commission on Ancient and Historic Monuments of Scotland recorded over 350 prehistoric and historic monuments within six miles of the village of Kilmartin, in the heart of Mid Argyll. Much of this work made use of material gathered by local antiquarians Marion Campbell and Mary Sandeman two decades earlier. And some task it was, for the sheer number of prehistoric monuments found here is extraordinary. But it is not only the number of sites and monuments that makes the area

[1]The Dalriada Project partners were Argyll and Bute Council, British Waterways Scotland, Forestry Commission Scotland, Kilmartin Museum, Scottish Natural Heritage and the Waterways Trust Scotland.

special; it is also the particular kinds of monuments: cairns, standing stones, stone circles and rock art that attest to the Glen's ritual significance in prehistory. In addition, many of the monuments are significant in their own right, and none more so than Dunadd Fort, home of the Kings of Dál Riata, a Kingdom that played a significant role in the creation of the Scottish nation.

The area is special too for a unique combination of flora and fauna. Some have described the woodlands as a temperate rainforest or, more romantically, a Celtic Rainforest. Indeed, it does rain rather a lot! But, rain aside, nowhere else can you walk through ancient oak woods dripping with lichens, mosses and ferns and take in wonderful views out over a sea punctuated with islands; or see views that shift constantly in the ever changing light. The diverse environments of Argyll are a wildlife haven for many species of mammals, birds, butterflies and invertebrates; some of these are very rare and/ or threatened species. There are two National Nature Reserves to explore, Taynish Atlantic Oak Woods, and the Mòine Mhór, a unique place where peat bog gradually changes into salt marsh. There are many other places of natural heritage interest too.

Kilmartin Museum

In the 1990s an idea emerged that there should be a visitor centre and museum located in Kilmartin Glen. The focus was to celebrate both the archaeology and natural history, and to create a place where some of the internationally important artefacts excavated from local archaeological sites could be displayed and enjoyed by locals and visitors. To that end, Kilmartin House Trust was formed by Rachel Butter and David Clough. Following a gruelling amount of hard work and fund raising, the Museum, café and shop opened to great acclaim.

More than 15 years on, and several funding crises later, the Museum survives and is thriving. We have funding agreements with Argyll and Bute Council and Historic Scotland, which provide around half of the funding needed to run our core services. The rest we generate ourselves from Museum ticket sales and the profits from the shop and café, but we continue to rely on donations of money and time. We are extremely grateful to our team of volunteers who give freely of their time to assist in so many ways.

The Museum aims to educate people about the past and we have in recent years consolidated our cultural and natural heritage education service and secured funding for this from Argyll and Bute Council, Forestry Commission Scotland, Historic Scotland, Scottish Natural Heritage and the Robertson Trust. We offer formal education to school age children, and informal workshops, events and courses, to help people enjoy and learn about the natural and cultural riches of the area. The service is enjoyed by adults and children alike. In addition, we support local artists and craftspeople by making their work available in the Museum shop and via exhibitions.

We feel that an archaeological museum should actively find out more about the prehistory and history of the area, putting into context the objects that it cares for. To this end we have engaged in a series of surveys during the last eight years and these have resulted in 450 more sites being recorded. Some of these were found during the course of our work, others were known by the landowners but not reported to the National Monument Record for Scotland. Our excavations have added to the continually emerging body of work about the area, as well as discovering new and exciting artefacts. You can find out more about this work on the Museum's website.

The dream that Kilmartin Museum would be a place where local archaeological objects could be cared for and interpreted is an enduring reality. We now collect and care for all of the archaeological objects that are found, by chance or excavation, in Mid Argyll and Kintyre. Kintyre artefacts can be seen in our sister museum in Campbeltown, which is owned by Argyll and Bute Council. This is our most important role, for if things are not collected and curated, then future generations will not be able to enjoy and be inspired by the objects and the people who created them thousands of years ago. Some artefacts from this area are part of the collections of the National Museum of Scotland, the British Museum, and Kelvingrove Museum, but many can be seen at Kilmartin. Visitors and locals alike are able to appreciate these artefacts in the Museum gallery, and they are able to step outside into the landscape to enjoy the sites and monuments where they were found.

Those of us who are lucky enough to live and work in and around this internationally significant landscape today are aware on a daily basis of what a special place it is. This book aims to help you explore the landscape and its cultural and natural riches, via a series of walking routes. But it is not just a walking guide – for we hope that it will also help you understand how the landscape has been shaped by the people who have lived here over the last 13,000 or so years and perhaps you will begin to understand how they, in turn, have been shaped by it.

So come, walk with us In the Footsteps of Kings and experience the magic of this place for yourself.

PART I

MID ARGYLL'S ARCHAEOLOGICAL AND HISTORICAL PAST

THE ICE AGE INTO THE BRONZE AGE

Reading the Landscape

Archaeologists, historians, geographers and geologists use various techniques to read the landscape and the monuments within it, allowing us to piece together its history so that we can understand how people lived there in the past, and how they made sense of their world. Sometimes this is challenging and there are questions that we will never know the answers to. Many prehistoric monuments were excavated by Victorian antiquarians, particularly so in Kilmartin Glen. Although they may have been working to a high standard at the time, many of the scientific techniques in use today were not available then, so information and some artefacts have been lost. More recent archaeological work undertaken in the area has added to this body of knowledge. There is, however, much more to explore.

Archaeologists may value the landscape for its ability to tell stories of the past, but there are other values embedded in it too. The land has always been a source of wealth, but in modern times activities such as forestry, wind farms and quarrying can sometimes conflict with the values of those seeking clues to the area's heritage, with those who enjoy the landscape for its natural beauty, and businesses who rely on tourism. Somehow, we must balance all these conflicting values and uses of the landscape, and remember that we all have a responsibility to ensure that future generations are able to enjoy the unique beauty of Mid Argyll, with its rich cultural and natural heritage.

Sculpted by Ice and Water

Around 23,000 to 20,000 years ago the last ice age was at its height, and Scotland was covered by a sheet of ice up to 400 metres thick in places. The ice was not static; it moved slowly, dragging boulders and rocks along its bottom, eroding the bedrock, scraping and etching the rock in places which can still be seen today.

Sea levels were lower because so much water was locked up in the ice. When the ice began to melt, sea levels rose rapidly, as did the land, for it was freed from the great weight of ice. Eventually the rising land caught up with the

Nether Largie Standing Stones (walk 1)

sea levels and so by 12,000 – 11,000 years ago, sea levels had fallen again, leaving the earlier coastlines higher in the landscape. As the ice left Scotland, herbs and grasses began to colonise, but not long after, the climate worsened and ice began to form once again. Although we are not sure of the extent of this ice, it is possible there were glaciers as far west as Loch Awe. These, and earlier glaciers, had fed the meltwater rivers which cascaded down Kilmartin Glen, depositing accumulations of silt and gravel along its course, forming flat topped terraces which, along with the traces of raised beaches, can be clearly seen in both Kilmartin and Kilmichael Glens today.

This cold period ended around 10,000 years ago with a very rapid rise in temperatures. Plants once again colonised; grasses and herbs being the first, followed by birch, hazel, oak and elm, and then animal life, which colonised each suitable habitat in the wake of plants.

First Peoples
Towards the end of the Upper Palaeolithic (Old Stone Age) and into the Mesolithic (Middle Stone Age) Period

Archaeologists think that the earliest evidence we had of people living in Argyll dated from around 9800 BC in the period archaeologists call the Mesolithic. However a remarkable discovery made in a cave at Kilmelford in the 1950s has been re-analysed and is changing that view. The finds were flint tools and waste flakes of a distinctive kind which suggested that humans might have been living in Argyll as early as 11000 BC, in the Upper Palaeolithic period, before the last retreat of ice from Scotland. Perhaps the tools were made by a group of hunters using the cave as shelter, having taken advantage of a warmer interval to move into the rich hunting grounds of the north? It is not surprising that we have so little evidence since the severe climatic conditions would have obliterated most traces of human occupation.

During the Mesolithic period, people lived by hunting, gathering and fishing, and they thrived on the rich larder of plants and animals. Deer, boar, and maybe even bear, were eaten. Bone was used for tools, sinew for string and binding, fur and skins for clothes. Many of the forest plants – mushrooms, berries, nuts and leaves – were edible, while others could have been used for medicine, and as materials for baskets, rope, and clothing. Wood from trees was important, and we can be sure that good use was made of the varying properties of different trees.

Stone, particularly flint, was an important raw material for making tools. Skills were sophisticated; for example, small flint tools that archaeologists call microliths were set into arrow shafts and held in place with a kind of glue, perhaps made from birch bark pitch.

As with later peoples, life would have revolved around water as much as land, for the inland lochs and sheltered seas around the coasts of Argyll would have been rich hunting grounds for seals, shellfish, fish, seaweeds, and water fowl. Boats might have taken the form of currachs. These fragile willow framed, skin covered vessels might have carried people around the coasts and islands to find seasonal food sources, collect special kinds of stone, and to allow them to gather together to swap stories, meet friends, relatives, and partners.

Argyll had everything they needed to live a reasonably comfortable life, but it could also be harsh at times, for predators capable of harming humans also roamed the land and seasonal food shortages would have had to be overcome.

The evidence we find is only a fraction of the suite of material culture these folk were capable of creating; many of their objects, tools and clothing would have been made from organic materials that do not usually survive. People did not live in permanent settlements; rather, they moved around using resources seasonally, sheltering in caves and creating temporary camps – the ephemeral remains of which might not have lasted a lifetime, let alone survive thousands of years. Yet traces of these people have been found. In Argyll their presence is most evident on the islands of Colonsay and Oronsay where pits of hazel nuts have been found, as well as shell middens – evidence of what people ate and discarded. Caves around Oban were excavated in the 19th century, revealing stone, bone and antler tools from this period. In Mid Argyll, a small pit filled with charcoal and a small flint tool was excavated at the Upper Largie Quarry site.

By the end of this period, the Argyll mainland would have been densely wooded, the upper and mid slopes of the hills cloaked in oak, ash, hazel and elm, with alder in the more boggy spots and birch where the soils were thinner. Today, this area is well known for its native woodlands, which support a dense variety of lichens, mosses and ferns as well as animal life. Although humans have been managing these for generations, it is not hard to imagine what life might have been like for the prehistoric hunter gatherers in the woods of Argyll 9,000 years ago.

Walks 15, 16 and 22 take you through some of the area's best examples of the 'Celtic rainforests' of Argyll.

People lived this way for thousands of years in a relatively stable system – yet, eventually, things changed.

Breaking the Earth
The Neolithic (New Stone Age)

Around 11,000 years ago, thousands of miles to the east of Argyll, change was afoot. People began to rely less and less on gathering wild resources, hunting and fishing. To begin with, cereal crops were planted and, later, animals were domesticated; first goats and sheep, then cattle. Settled communities with permanent houses were built. This new way of life is known as the 'Neolithic', and the change that it represents is arguably the most fundamental that humans have undergone as a species.

These changes spread throughout Europe; they are detected in the archaeological record in Britain from at least as early as 6,000 years ago, thousands of years after they were first seen in the near east. Previously unknown cereal crops and animals spread north and westwards, but the uptake of a farming lifestyle was not uniform. Theories abound on the reasons why this change took place – nor are the mechanisms well understood. Arguments have been made for the spread of farming being either a movement of ideas or movement of people. It seems likely that the onset of the Neolithic was a combination of the two. Communities adapted, and adopted varying ways of making a living from the land to suit their particular environmental conditions. Some people moved into new areas while reliance on wild resources might have continued. But, eventually, everyone in Scotland adopted this lifestyle.

As animals were domesticated from their wild forms, people had access not only to meat and skins, but also milk. Wool from sheep could also have been used. Cereal crops such as wheat, barley, and other plants were grown. Evidence for this comes from pollen, charred grains and from saddle querns made of stone used to grind grain. Wild resources continued to be important. In Kilmichael Glen evidence has been found of cereals dating to this period. In other parts of Argyll we have little evidence of Neolithic activity. It is possible that change came slower to some areas, but some traces are very hard to find without extensive excavation.

New kinds of stone tools were in use at this time, including ground stone axes and leaf shaped arrowheads. Some of the stone was found locally, but some was imported – evidence of long range contacts. For example, two stone axes which are now in Kilmartin Museum were found in North Knapdale. These were made from a type of stone that comes from Northern Ireland. Ground stone axes could have been used for chopping down trees to clear forest for fields, and to acquire timber; they could also be used to butcher animals, and as weapons. These objects also had symbolic 'lives', circulating amongst different folk, creating obligations and ties, while a few came to be regarded as sacred objects.

Pottery was a new innovation during the Neolithic period in Britain and it enabled people to cook, store and serve food in ways that would not have been possible before. But like many objects during this time, it also had symbolic significance, and as well as being used for domestic purposes; pots were often buried with the dead. Some pots were highly decorated, with patterns that reveal regional and local styles, creating a sense of community amongst people in a particular area, but also a sense of difference. Pottery from this period can be seen in Kilmartin Museum.

Clearing forest, preparing ground and building houses represented an investment in a place, and would have tied people to a particular area. At this time there were also profound changes in the way that people made sense of the world around them, and their relationship to the land, which had an impact on the landscape; for it was at this time that people began to build monuments. In Kilmartin, around 3500 BC, a massive timber monument was erected on a gravel terrace at Upper Largie, the first evidence of Neolithic activity here. Archaeologists call this kind of monument a cursus, and it consisted of two lines of parallel lengths of posts that ran for nearly 400 metres; an imposing structure visible from a great distance. Cursus monuments are known in other parts of Scotland and various theories have been put forward to explain why they were built and what they were used for, including processional or ceremonial pathways. Others have suggested they might have acted as buffer zones between the worlds of the living and the dead, between ceremonial land and farmland. The cursus at Upper Largie was destroyed by fire. Some have suggested it was deliberately burned, an act that was more likely part of its purpose and a ceremony in its own right, rather than wanton destruction. The spectacle of the posts burning in a long line would have been a striking and dramatic event – especially so during the hours of darkness and in which case it would have been visible for miles. No traces of this monument, built and burned sometime between 3800 BC and 3650 BC, now exist; following excavation they have been quarried away.

We do not know for certain whether the ceremonies at the cursus marked the relationship between the living and the dead, but this is clearer at other monuments, for some were built to house the dead. Archaeologists call these chambered cairns, and similar cairns are found elsewhere in Western Europe. Some of these have been excavated, creating a large body of work from which

Inside Nether Largie South (walk 1)

we can piece together what these sites were used for.

Twenty or so chambered cairns are known in Mid Argyll, including Nether Largie South (walk 1) in Kilmartin Glen, all of a regional type known as Clyde Cairns, probably constructed around 3700 BC. These structures were built as places of communal burial, and were also probably the focus of ceremonies both inside and outside the tomb, creating a continued relationship between the living and the dead. The dead were placed inside, sometimes with grave goods, and once the flesh had fallen away, skeletal remains were often separated and segregated in different parts of the tomb. Grave goods, in the form of pottery and tools, were often placed inside. Some tombs, such as Maeshowe in Orkney and Newgrange in Ireland, were constructed so that sunlight could flood into the chamber at the midwinter solstice, the sun perhaps shining on the bones of the dead, linking the living and the dead and renewing life and ensuring fertility for the coming year.

The building of chambered cairns represents a big investment of time and energy for a small scale farming community. People may have required strategies to emphasise their 'ancestral' ties to particular pieces of land and their rights to use it, as well as being concerned with the relationship of the living to supernatural forces or 'otherworlds'. The performance of ceremonies and rituals within and around the monuments may have served to cement a group of people to a place, and to each other, in a common endeavour – literally creating a sense of community. But perhaps these acts also separated and defined differences between people, because it is not clear if everyone was afforded a burial inside a chambered cairn.

Towards the end of this period, in the late Neolithic, around 3000 BC, some 700 years after Nether Largie South Chambered Cairn was built, people constructed a new kind of monument – a timber circle – at Temple Wood (walk 1). This was replaced by a stone circle, and then another stone circle a little to the south west.

We can never know with absolute certainty what stone circles were used for, however it has been suggested that they might have been places of ceremony, where rites and rituals, or trade exchanges, might have been performed. Others have suggested they were used for measuring the movements of the sun and moon, to measure time and to predict farming events such as when to harvest crops – all very important events for a small scale farming society.

Marking the Land
Late Neolithic

Another means of transforming the landscape during this period was the practice of marking earthfast rocks – the very bones of the land – with motifs that we call rock art. Rock art can be found almost all over the world, but the particular suite of motifs found here have similarities with other sites in Britain, Ireland, and elsewhere along the Atlantic seaboard. Rock art does seem to have held a particular importance for the people living in Mid Argyll, for this area contains the greatest number of rock carvings of this period in the country and more sites are being discovered every year. Mid Argyll also has some of the most elaborate rock art sites; these include Cairnbaan (walk 14), Baluachraig (walk 6), Ormaig (walk 3), and Achnabreck, which is also the largest cup and ring marked rock sheet in Europe (walk 12). There are hundreds of less elaborate sites, with carvings appearing on outcropping bedrock, on boulders and on small portable stones. The most common motif found is a shallow circle known as a cup mark; sometimes there are more complex designs involving rings around the cup marks and other motifs. The designs were made by repeatedly 'pecking' the surface of a rock with a pointed tool made of a harder kind of stone than the surface being carved. In Kilmartin and Kilmichael Glens rock art also appears on stones

used in burial monuments, and on standing stones.

Establishing the antiquity of rock art has proved difficult, for living rock is hard to date. Recent excavations at the Torbhlaren rock art site (walk 11) found charcoal associated with hammerstones, and a radio carbon date of between 2920 BC and 2760 BC was obtained. Other work in Ireland has produced similar results, suggesting that rock art made on earthfast rocks is part of a late Neolithic tradition.

Dating rock art used in monuments is easier; for example, we can be sure that the flat axe motifs carved on stones used in some of the burial cists in Kilmartin Glen date to the Early Bronze Age – the same age as the monument. An argument has been made that cup and ring marked standing stones were once marked earthfast rocks, which were later quarried or dug up and erected as standing stones, to perhaps draw on the ancient power of these earlier monuments. Others have suggested the stones were quarried then carved, perhaps just before they were erected. You can see examples of rock art marked standing stones at Nether Largie (walk 1), Ballymeanoch (walk 6) and on a standing stone at Torbhlaren (walk 11).

Researchers have struggled to understand the reasons why

people created rock art, and what it meant to them. Non-specialists have made hundreds of suggestions, ranging from the somewhat flippant idea that it is mere graffiti to the speculation that the carvings might be maps of the stars, neither of which fit the evidence.

Archaeologists can reconstruct many aspects of people's lives, but aspects such as belief, ritual and religion are harder to understand. It is simply not possible to get inside the heads of prehistoric people, but we can perhaps get closer to an understanding by thorough study of the available evidence. Excavations around some sites in Scotland and Ireland have revealed that the rock art itself might have been only part of what was once at the site. Archaeologists have considered the landscape setting of these sites, and have studied other contemporary sites, monuments, and material culture. They have discussed rock art and painting with cultures that still make it; and through these various routes have been able to come closer to understanding rock art as part of prehistoric people's way of making sense of the world with a culture of monument building. Meaning probably changed over time, and may well have meant different things to different facets of a community. The act of creation may have been as important as the end result.

Cup and ring marks at Cairnbaan (walk 14)

New Ways, New People?
Chalcolithic (Copper Age)

Over time, burial tradition changed. In Kilmartin Glen we have evidence of this around 2500 BC, a period archaeologists call the Chalcolithic – when metal first made its appearance in Britain. On a terrace at Upper Largie (now a gravel quarry) a person was buried in a grave made for a single individual. Although archaeologists found no trace of a body, a pot and flint objects, placed as grave goods, were found. This type of grave, and the objects within, had never been seen in Scotland before and because of its apparent similarities to graves in the Lower Rhine region, some archaeologists believe that this was the grave of a Continental immigrant, who may have travelled to the area because of the copper deposits here. The pot found in the grave is of a kind known as a 'Beaker', and it was at this time that this

Beaker from Temple Wood

and other novelties such as the knowledge of metal working were making their appearance in Britain and Ireland.

Expressions of the Elite:
The Early Bronze Age

By about 2200 BC, probably about three centuries after copper and gold came into use, bronze (an alloy of tin and copper) made its appearance in Scotland. The people who could undertake the transformation of dull rock to shiny, hard metal might well have been regarded as magicians or shamans, and its use may well have transformed society too, for demand for metal objects was high and those who were able to control the flow of this material became powerful. It has been suggested that the people living in Kilmartin Glen were able to do this on a large scale over a wide area. This then enabled the development of an elite, who were able to express their status through the construction of very conspicuous burial monuments – a series of massive cairns in a line down Kilmartin Glen, now known as the linear cemetery (walk 1). Five cairns survive today; the Glebe Cairn, Nether Largie North Cairn, Nether Largie Mid Cairn, Ri Cruin and the earlier Nether Largie South Cairn, which was at this time transformed to resemble the others. Records from a few hundred years ago indicate a sixth cairn, the stones of which were completely removed, probably to build roads and walls.

The cairns generally consist of a cist (the Gaelic word for chest) – a stone slab–built box–like chamber, which was sealed by a capping slab and cairn material (water rolled cobbles) heaped over the top. Some of the slabs used to build the cists were carved with images of flat axes – representations perhaps of the source of the elite's status? There are other cairns in the hills of Kilmartin Glen and elsewhere in Mid Argyll, but nowhere else in Scotland is there a similar arrangement of cairns as in the linear cemetery which stretches for some miles down Kilmartin Glen.

Not everyone was afforded such status in death, and other more simple burials from this period are known.

Status was also expressed through objects – such as necklaces and bracelets made of jet and sometimes cannel coal. Necklaces are generally found in the graves of high status women. The nearest source of jet is some 300 miles on foot to the south east in Whitby, Yorkshire. Prehistoric people may have understood it to have magical properties – for although it looks like stone, it is semi-fossilised wood and so it floats, can burn, and has electrostatic properties. Two such necklaces have been found in Kilmartin Glen.

Beakers continued to be used alongside new styles of pottery,

Jet necklace from Campbeltown Museum

©Aaron Watson/Campbeltown Museum

which have similarities to Irish pottery – they are known as Food Vessels and some believe they were made by specialist Irish potters, rather than the designs having been copied. One such pot found in a grave on the Upper Largie gravel terrace is unique to Scotland, its body being an Irish style 'Food Vessel', but it has four short clay legs, a feature of Food Vessels found in Yorkshire.

As well as adapting the earlier chambered cairn at Nether Largie South, the Early Bronze Age people of Kilmartin also reworked the South West circle at Temple Wood, using it for burial, and possibly dismantled the North East Circle; and there are tantalising suggestions that they might have reused the stones in other monuments. This is the case elsewhere in Mid Argyll; at Badden, near Lochgilphead, stone carved with Late Neolithic lozenge shaped designs was reused in a cist.

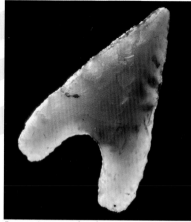

Bronze Age arrowhead

Other monuments too might date to this period.

People still continued to farm in much the same way as in earlier periods. Wild plants and animals might still have been important. People continued to use stone to make tools, but some of the types of tools changed; for example, barbed and tanged arrowheads were used – the culmination of centuries of people learning to manipulate flint.

Time in Stone
Middle and Later Bronze Age

People continued to use the Glen as a place of burial over the next few centuries, into the period archaeologists know as the Middle Bronze Age. They constructed new kinds of burial monuments called 'kerb-cairns' and the ashes of cremated people were interred here. They built other monuments too; between 1600 BC and 1400 BC, a massive timber circle was erected on the Upper Largie gravel terrace and, between 1400 BC and 1050 BC, standing stones were set in rows at Ballymeanoch (walk 6). Probably at the same time, a more complex row was set at Nether Largie. Both seem to mark the position of the sun and moon, possibly at various astronomical events.

By about 1000 BC it appears that ritual activity ceased in Kilmartin Glen. There is evidence for later activity nearby – for example, the discovery of a late Bronze Age metal work hoard at Torran, on the shore of Loch Awe.

While we have a large body of evidence of ritual and burial activity in Kilmartin Glen, there is very little evidence of settlement. Some have argued that people were not living in the Glen, rather, it was an area reserved for ritual, but evidence of domestic dwellings would be very hard to find since such buildings might not leave upstanding traces. Evidence from Kilmichael Glen demonstrates that cereals were still being grown there, indicating that land used for monuments was also used for farming.

The life histories of the prehistoric monuments in Mid Argyll are complicated, and are still undergoing transformations of meaning, a process that will no doubt continue to unfold as new research is undertaken.

THE IRON AGE INTO THE HISTORIC PERIOD

A Defended Landscape

By about 800 BC, changes were afoot in Scotland. The ways that people made sense of the world around them were transformed and old ritual and burial sites were abandoned, perhaps in favour of rites and rituals that have left little trace. All over Europe many hilltops were being fortified, a process that began there considerably earlier than in Scotland. A new kind of metal was in use – iron – far harder than bronze, and more easily forged into an array of different tools and weapons. The raw materials were more readily available too, so old trade routes might have been disrupted or become redundant altogether.

In Argyll there is evidence that the climate slowly cooled and became wetter, resulting in changes in the vegetation. Probably towards the end of the Bronze Age, peat began to form and expand up Kilmartin Glen – this has become known as the Mòine Mhór (Great Moss, walk 8). Gradually standing stones and other earlier monuments were partially covered with peat, especially those towards Crinan Estuary. As the climate worsened, land that had been productive for farming was lost.

In Scotland by about 800 BC people were constructing what we now call crannogs, artificial or partially artificial islands, mainly on inland lochs. Wood was a valuable building commodity; used for houses and to make many different kinds of utensils, tools, and vessels. Most of these objects have decayed, but in the cold peaty waters of Scotland's lochs some have survived, along with parts of the structure of the crannog itself. This comparative wealth of evidence means that we know quite a lot about the life of people living in such buildings. In Argyll, excavations on the Loch Glashan crannog revealed a rich group of objects, albeit from a later period, which demonstrated that crannogs, as a style of building, were used for a long period of time. There are many other crannogs in the area, for example Loch Awe alone is thought to have more than 20. None of these have been fully excavated; one structure on nearby Loch Ederline has been briefly examined.

Crannogs were not principally defensive, but may have relied on being surrounded by water for protection. Other buildings relied on the strength of stone, and archaeologists have classified these structures as duns, forts and brochs. All of these are regional variants of the 'Scottish Atlantic Round House' tradition. Brochs are large stone towers with internal galleries.

Mostly found in the north and north east of the country, a broch is a building type that hardly made inroads into Argyll, with only one known in the district, this being Tirefour on the Island of Lismore.

Nearly 100 duns and forts have been recorded in Mid Argyll. Both types of building are defined by stone walls. Forts are larger in size than duns, and sometimes have outworks along with internal structures. Some forts were built with timber laced stone walls, which on occasion caught fire – either by accident, or, as is more probable, deliberate burning. The build up of heat from these fires could be so intense that the stone of the walls literally fused, leading to the term 'vitrified fort'. Duns (Dùn is a Gaelic word meaning fort, fortified site or hill) were generally built on hilltops, and are circular or oval in plan – the walls often follow the natural topography. Some sites might have been little more than look-out points, while others were more elaborate, with galleries, and steps leading to wall heads. Most were probably roofed with timber and thatch; others may have had internal structures built inside the sheltering walls.

All these different kinds of building, including crannogs, were built near tracts of fertile farm land. Crops similar to the previous period would have been grown, and cattle were the main source of meat, but also a symbol of wealth and prestige. There were still many areas of woodland during this period, and people probably continued to hunt wild animals for fur and meat. Fish, shellfish and wild plants would have been collected for food, medicines and materials.

Although there is a large body of evidence from the north east of Scotland and the Outer Isles from this period, in Argyll, with the exception of a couple of major excavations, there has been comparatively little work done. We can determine, however, that Argyll's forts, duns and crannogs were probably in use from about 2,500 years ago and in some cases were occupied, or reoccupied, throughout the medieval period, into the 17th century in some cases.

More recent work by Kilmartin Museum at Barnluasgan and Balure Duns in Knapdale has gained carbon dates from 230 – 20 BC, demonstrating Iron Age occupation. On both sites the upper half of decorated rotary querns were discovered, and at Barnluasgan some charred cereal grains were found. The cereals would have been ground into meal on these, or similar, quern stones. At Balure evidence of metalworking was also found. Other finds included glass beads – suggesting that the site

Castle Dounie (walk 17)

Glass beads from Balure Dun

was occupied by someone of high status.

As well as being close to land suitable for farming, duns and forts appear to have been strategically placed in the landscape to overlook both overland and sea routes, and thus it is likely their occupants were controlling territory. Fortified sites were probably the residence of local leaders and prominent families. There might have been other forms of habitation. We know undefended huts existed elsewhere to accommodate people of lower status and this could have been the case in Argyll too. While we can never be sure what social, cultural and political factors led to the building of these sites, major events happening in the rest of Britain and Europe are sure to have played a part. The Romans first invaded southern Britain in AD 43, eventually gaining control of a large part of the country. Argyll was never occupied by their forces, but the threat of invasion must have been a constant concern for its indigenous inhabitants, perhaps especially so during the Roman

naval operations that took place in western waters in the later decades of the 1st century AD. The Romans might have been regarded as a threat, but they were also a source of exotic goods, including pottery, glass beads, and drinking vessels. Historical events demonstrate there was a need for defence but the building of stone tower–like structures might also have served as status symbols; a visible demonstration of strength and power.

Some of the earliest written accounts of Scotland exist from this time. These sources were written by outsiders with a political agenda, and so should be treated with a degree of caution; however, they afford tantalising glimpses of a tribal society where warrior elites were the dominant force. Ptolemy, a Roman citizen living in the 2nd century AD, describes the Kintyre peninsula as being the territory of the Epidii, and their northern neighbours were the Creones or Cerones.

Unlike earlier periods, we find little evidence of Iron Age people's treatment of the dead. Whichever gods and goddesses were worshipped, their beliefs were not manifested in the building of stone monuments. A tantalising glimpse of Iron Age beliefs was found in Northern Argyll in the 19th century when a carved wooden figure was found preserved in peat. This may have been a votive offering, or a representation of a deity[1].

The Kingdom of Dál Riata
The 5th century AD to the 10th century AD

By the beginning of the 5th century AD, Roman rule in Britain and Southern Scotland was at an end. Historians define this as the beginning of the early historic period, but in Argyll there is no convenient cut off date between the Iron Age and the Roman Period, so the exact beginning of the early historic period is a matter of some debate. For the people living in Argyll, life might have gone on much as usual – we have no sense of how the withdrawal of Roman rule in the east and south would have affected them. Nor do we know much about the evolution of the various ethnic and cultural groups that had emerged by the beginning of the 5th century AD, but from this time on, more archaeological and historical evidence is available.

Between the 5th and 10th centuries AD, Scotland was home to many different peoples and cultures, including Picts, Britons, Scotti, Gaels, Angles, and later the Norse (or Vikings). Some of these names would not have been recognised by the people who were described

thus, for they are derived from external sources. The profusion of terms hints at the complexities and entanglements involved in trying to understand ethnicity and its relationship with material culture and language in Scotland at this time. Certainly by the 6th century AD, perhaps earlier, the Picts had emerged as a separate cultural and ethnic identity in the north east of Scotland. This name had previously been used in the 3rd century AD in classical sources, but possibly as an insult, and the people described thus might not have had any relationship to the Picts of the 6th century AD.

The term 'Pict' was not applicable along the western seaboard in the 6th century AD, for this was the home of another group of people, who had their own distinctive cultural identity. Because they spoke Gaelic they are often referred to as Gaels, but they are also known as the Scotti. This term was used by Latin writers to refer to both Irish and Scots Gaelic speakers, and it probably isn't very flattering. Although it is tempting to call the inhabitants of Argyll the earliest Scots in Scotland, it is probably best to use the term Gael, as it is an approximation of what they called themselves. In the context of Argyll, it is probably equally acceptable, if not the general convention, to describe them as 'the Dál Riata'.

[1] This is known as the Ballachulish Figure, and it is on display in the National Museum of Scotland.

In a maelstrom of shifting alliances, territorial struggles, and warring kin groups, people and events occurring in Argyll were a major factor in the emergence of the nation of Scotland, for, between about 600 and 900 AD, these people had established what is now one of the most significant monuments for the whole Scottish nation, the Royal fortress of Dunadd; centre of the Kingdom of Dál Riata.

Many kingdoms hark back to a heroic ancestor in their origin myths. The Dál Riata were no different, for they ascribed the founding of the Kingdom in Scotland to Fergus Mór mac Eirc, a Gael living in Co. Antrim in Ireland, who invaded Argyll in 500 AD. The story comes from the 'Miniuguid Senchusa fher nAlban', the 'History of the Men of Scotland'; a 10th century manuscript which incorporates material from the mid 7th century. Although the account described in this document is simplified, written and possibly rewritten with political motivations, elements are almost certainly true. Events relating to Argyll are also described in the Annals of Ulster. These, and other sources, have provided historians with a wealth of information, albeit subject to interpretation.

Recent research suggests that the migration of the Gaels of Dál Riata might not have been a large scale single event whereby Irish people moved to Scotland. Contact between the two peoples had a long history. The same Gaelic language was spoken on both sides of the Irish Sea. This is, after all, a narrow expanse of water that, far from being a barrier, was an easy means of connecting the two lands at a time when travel by boat was by far the swiftest form of transport. It has been suggested that in fact it was Scottish Gaels who moved into Ireland to found the Kingdom of Dál Riata.

The fascinating story of Dunadd has been revealed through several excavations, the most recent being undertaken by Ewan Campbell and Alan Lane in the 1980s. The excavations revealed some amazing artefacts, and although these are now part of the collections of the National Museum of Scotland, many have been loaned to Kilmartin Museum, where they can be seen in the context of the landscape in which they were found.

The rocky crag of Dunadd had already been fortified in the Iron Age. During the 300 – 400 years that the Kingdom existed here, the fortifications were modified and many new buildings added. Dunadd became a major political centre, making diplomatic contacts, and sometimes political alliances, with all the other major kingdoms of the day. But this was also a warrior culture. The Kings of Dál Riata intermittently engaged in warfare with their neighbours, the Picts of the north and east, and the Britons and Angles who occupied territories in other parts of northern Britain. Later, too, there were conflicts with the Norse who were notorious for raiding along the Scottish and Irish seaboards, but who also settled in Scotland, especially in the islands. The Dál Riata also fought amongst themselves. During the early years of the Kingdom, lands were held by the Norse in Argyll and also in Antrim in Northern Ireland; the latter may have been ruled from Scotland. Later, these territories were separated and Scotland became a separate political entity.

Dunadd was also a centre of trade which imported many exotic goods, including spices and wines. Pottery from France has been found here, which contained traces of madder – a plant that can be used to make a rich red dye. We do not know what was exported, possibly fish or furs hunted from the extensive woodlands of Argyll. Slaves were a valuable commodity at the time, and it is possible they were one of the exports from Argyll. Small ships, or shallow drafted boats, might have negotiated their way up the River Add to the base of the rock to bring goods from the harbour at Crinan to the regional capital, connecting the Kings of Dál Riata to the rest of Europe. This was a Kingdom reliant on sea routes.

At the same time, Christianity was beginning to take hold in Scotland. There would have been extensive contact between Dunadd and Iona, then one of the most important Christian centres in western Europe. It is likely that monks or priests were living at Dunadd, a speculation fuelled by the discovery of orpiment, a pigment used in the production of illuminated manuscripts – religious books that were highly decorated. The most famous surviving example of an illuminated manuscript is the fabulously decorative Book of Kells, now in Trinity College Dublin, which is thought to have been made on Iona.

The excavations found evidence that people worked with gold, silver, bronze and iron. The production of metal objects would have been under the control of the King. Weapons were made here, as is to be expected of such a warrior society, and items of jewellery were created. The giving of gifts – brooches in particular – would have been one way of symbolically sealing alliances. Through these alliances the King established fealty, extracted tribute in the form of cattle or grain, and raised fighting men and ships if needed; an early form of tax collection.

At Dunadd, the brooches themselves have not survived, but hundreds of fragments of clay brooch moulds have been found revealing (in reverse) bird headed decoration and interlaced work. Other leaders may have sent gifts too, for Anglo Saxon objects were found at the site. Evidently there was time for leisure, for gaming board pieces were also found.

Such a busy place would have needed food. The land around Dunadd would have been farmed – cereal grains, including one of the earliest finds of oats, which became an important food source, have been identified here. Cereals were processed with quern stones – also found at the site. The bones of cattle, sheep and pigs reveal the importance of meat, milk and wool. Cattle might have been a symbol of wealth, as they were in earlier times.

Dunadd was home to a warrior elite, and a stronghold from which to launch campaigns, but it was also a symbolic and ritual centre where Kings were literally made. Kingship in early medieval Scotland was somewhat different from today – a suitable man was chosen from a group of eligible nobles; political abilities and prowess in battle as important, perhaps, as their lineage. Rocks near the summit of Dunadd have been carved with footprints, a rock cut basin and a boar. They are thought to have been used in the inauguration ceremonies that conferred kingly status upon an individual. The Dál Riata may have had other strongholds – for example, Dunollie near Oban, Dunaverty in Kintyre and Dunagoil on Bute. The importance of these strongholds rose and fell with the prestige of their occupants. At times they were separate kingdoms, at others they were sub-kingdoms, subservient to whichever lineage was in the ascendancy at that time.

The combination of carvings, however, strengthens the assumption that Dunadd is the caput regionis (chief place of the region) described in the 7th century by Adomnán, a monk of Iona, in his biography of St Columba. The ritual is believed to have involved the new King placing his foot into the footprint carving, linking the land and the people. The inauguration of the Kings of Dál Riata may not have been an entirely pagan ritual. Adomnán describes how St Columba inaugurated Áedán mac Gabráin, so it appears that the Church had cleverly manoeuvred itself into a central role in these rituals – thus gaining a great deal of political power.

Religious men, often themselves from wealthy and elite families, might have been in control of the written word. This too held great power, as

The inauguration stone on Dunadd (walk 9)

few at the time had the ability to read. Histories, censuses and records could be kept in this way. Previously, important information would have been communicated orally and so the use of writing represented a profound change in the way that knowledge was held and transmitted. The religious and secular authorities thus reinforced and legitimised each other.

Although access to the sea was important, there might have been other more symbolic reasons for siting the Royal residence at Dunadd. Not only is the rock of Dunadd itself impressive and imposing, but from here, on a clear day, the boundaries of the Kingdom, represented by Cruachan, the Paps of Jura and the hills of Arran, are visible. Moreover, there might have been a deliberate and conscious effort to create a link to the prehistoric landscape, as if the later kings were drawing on the power and antiquity of these by now ancient monuments. A similar proximity to ancient sites has been noted at other Royal centres in Scotland.

By the 7th century AD the Dál Riata had become the controlling force in an area extending from Ardnamurchan to Arran. In the Kingdom of Dál Riata we can detect the beginnings of many of the trappings of state that we take for granted today, including tax collection, census taking and an organised military force.

People of the Cross

Christianity became increasingly important over this period and some individuals stand out as having played a major role in this. One such is St Columba (Colm Cille). Born in 521 AD, he was of Irish Royal descent, with close links to the Dál Riata. His status and links would have no doubt played a role in the founding of the monastery at Iona in 563 AD, for this island was part of the Kingdom of Dál Riata. Adomnán's biography of the Saint tells of his missions to the Picts in the north east, and of miraculous deeds. He is also credited with having brought Christianity to Scotland, but there is some exaggeration in Adomnán's work, and it is thought that the country was already Christian by the 6th century AD.

Protection and patronage played a part in the relationship between King and Church, evidence of which can be seen in the landscape today. There is a profusion of early ecclesiastical sites around Dunadd, which can be identified by the 'Kil' (meaning chapel, or church) element in a place name. Other evidence takes the form of a number of carved free standing crosses, as well as crosses and other religious symbols carved on earthfast rock. Objects associated with the Christian religion have also been found at Dunadd, including a quern stone carved with the form of the cross, and a stone disc dating to the 8th century AD, which has been carved with the letters 'inomine' the beginning of the Latin blessing 'in the name of the Father...'

Adomnán was also an Abbot of Iona and an important historical figure in his own right, writing the Law of the Innocents, one of the earliest declarations of human rights, aimed at protecting noncombatants in battle. This document, which Adomnán managed to persuade over 50 kings to endorse, demonstrates the influence of the Church, but also shows us that early medieval Scotland was a violent and conflict–ridden place.

By the 8th century AD Iona had become a major Christian centre. There were other religious houses in the area for both men and women, including an abbey on the Island of Lismore founded by Saint Moluag. There is also evidence of other Irish Saints in the area. Clergy were also known to have sought out isolated places for periods of contemplation and meditation and the islands and the isolated coastline of Argyll were ideally suited to this quest for solitude. As the Church developed, religious houses became larger, and some founded smaller dependencies nearby. Noble patronage was encouraged.

Clergy may well have come to minister to the lay population, preaching in the open air at a significant point in the landscape as well as in small chapels. The local population, too, might have visited monasteries, perhaps to pay penance or respect to the bones or relics of a saint. Carved crosses were erected, to commemorate a saint or important local person, a tradition that continued well into the later medieval period. Argyll has a wealth of carved crosses and grave slabs, some beautifully decorated with interlaced knot work that we now think of as classically 'Celtic' in style; which is also found in jewellery and illuminated manuscripts. These designs were perhaps intended to draw the viewer into a state of contemplation so that they might reach a state that would bring them closer to the power of Christ.

Raiders from the North

Towards the end of the 8th century AD a new group of people began making their presence felt in a series of violent raids around the coasts of Britain and Ireland. They were, of course, the Norse (or Vikings as they are sometimes known). The Norse raids were motivated at first by the acquisition of portable valuables, and in this endeavour they targeted wealthy monasteries and seriously disrupted monastic life. The first raid on Iona is recorded in 794, and, from then on the Norse were a constant threat, resulting ultimately in the abandonment of the Abbey in the early 9th century AD. The remaining relics were taken to Ireland in the west and to Dunkeld in the east for safekeeping.

By the early 9th century various branches of the Dál Riata held territory in Argyll and the Inner Hebrides. The Norse had also begun to settle, particularly on the islands, and are likely to have intermarried into the local populations. They also became Christian and engaged in trade.

The Kingdom moves East

By the mid 9th century AD, the Dál Riata dynasty had begun to expand into the Pictish Kingdom. Eventually, the two Kingdoms were united under a Gaelic speaking ruler, Cináed mac Alpín (Kenneth MacAlpin). It has been suggested that the Norse attacks had weakened the Pictish Kingdom in the east, allowing Cináed mac Alpín to take control and unify two once warring groups. The Norse might have been an element in the decision to move the power centre from its heartland at Dunadd in the west to Forteviot in the east, but this move might also have been a conscious step away from the old power centre of the Gaels. Although Dunadd ceased to be the capital, it retained symbolic significance and continued to be occupied to some degree into later centuries.

A Time of Chaos?[2]
The 9th century to the 11th century

Understanding the nature of society and culture along the western seaboard of Scotland in the 9th and 10th centuries and the early decades of the 11th century is problematic – there are few documentary sources, and little direct archaeological evidence. We do not know what replaced the power base when it moved from Dunadd, or if the united Dál Riata-Pictish Kings retained control over part of their former western territory. People of Norse descent were probably ruling the islands and parts of the mainland. As in earlier periods, a strong leader might have brought these territories together, but at other times they would have been ruled by a profusion of different chiefs and there would have been a good deal of infighting. By the 10th century the Kingdom known in Gaelic as Alba, and in English as Scotland, had emerged, but it is uncertain how much of Argyll was part of this Kingdom.

Along the west coast and islands during this time a

[2]As this summary progresses through the early historic period into the medieval and early modern period it is increasingly summarised for the reasons stated in the introduction. See the end of the book and our website for suggestions for further reading which will enable you to gain a fuller picture of the complexities and conflicts involved in this history.

new identity was beginning to emerge from people who had mixed ethnic and cultural backgrounds, the origins of which, to varying degrees, were Gaelic, Pictish, and Scandinavian (as well as British and Anglian). Describing the fusion of Gaelic and Scandinavian art styles historians use the term Hiberno-Norse, and this has sometimes been applied to people as well.

Parts of Argyll were at times under Scandinavian rule. One story appears in the Sagas of how in 1098, Norse leader Magnus Barelegs cleverly won Kintyre and the Islands from the Scottish King who had agreed that Magnus would rule all the territories that he could sail his longship around. Magnus ordered his men to drag his boat over the narrow isthmus at Tarbert and thus gained the Kintyre Peninsula. As well as Norse influence in the area, links to Ireland remained strong.

A New Leader Emerges
The 12th and 13th centuries

By the middle of the 12th century a new dynasty was emerging from this mixed Norse and Gaelic culture, under the leadership of Somerled (Somhairle mac Gillebrigte), and this was to become the Lordship of the Isles. Probably born into one of the leading noble families Somerled became a leader at a time when the Scottish crown

was being contested. He married into the Norwegian King of the Isles family, and eventually gained territory – either through military action, or political manoeuvring - in mainland Argyll and the Isles. He held this from about 1158 to his death in 1164. Somerled was succeeded by his sons and grandsons. At times they owed allegiance to the Scottish and Norwegian Kings, at other times Ireland, but some also fought fiercely with each other. Later descendants were the progenitors of the MacDougalls, the MacDonalds and MacRuaris, together known as the MacSorleys.

The first medieval castles were built during this time, these buildings being square in plan, with strong curtain walls enclosing other buildings. Castle Sween dates to this period (walk 24) and it is one of the oldest stone castles on the western mainland.

Towards the end of the century the diocese of Argyll was formed, under the See of Dunkeld, with its cathedral being on Lismore. Other chapels were built at this time, including Keills (walk 23) which is thought to date to the later part of the 12th century.

Somerled's descendants, the MacDonalds, based themselves at Finlaggan on Islay. They were semi-autonomous from the Scottish crown, which did

not initially recognise the title. Indeed, they themselves appeared not to have much respect for the Scottish Crown, for they and the MacSweens supported the Norwegian King Magnus's invasion of Scotland. Magnus was defeated by the Scottish King Alexander III at the Battle of Largs in 1263. For the part they had played in the failed invasion, in 1264 the MacSweens lost the castles of Skipness and Sween, the latter to the Stewart Earls of Menteith.

Thereafter, the descendants of Somerled became increasingly, and perhaps reluctantly, integrated into the Scottish nobility. In 1293 King John had created two sheriffdoms, Lorn, which was held by Alexander MacDougall, which extended from Ardnamurchan to Knapdale. The other, Kintyre, was held by the Stewart Earls of Menteith, who became Lords of Knapdale. Noble families in the area became caught up in the conflict between King John Balliol and Robert the Bruce. The MacDougalls remained loyal to the Balliol King, but lost their principal residence, Dunstaffnage Castle, in 1321 or 1322 following its capture by Robert the Bruce.

Other castles were constructed at this time. For example, Fincharn, at the southern end of Loch Awe, is thought to have existed by the mid–13th century. Duntrune Castle might also have

been partly built at this time. As well as castles, several chapels which may date to this century were constructed, possibly replacing earlier buildings, including Kilmory (walk 25), Kilmarie (walk 4), Kilbride and Kilneuair. Other medieval chapels undoubtedly existed at Kilmartin and Kilmichael Glassary, but these have been replaced by later buildings.

Lords of the Isles
The 14th century

The early years of the 14th century in Scotland were turbulent – conflict known as the wars of independence raged between supporters of Robert the Bruce and Edward Balliol, King John's son. The politics of this period were complicated, with leading Argyll families trying to protect or advance their own interests, often switching sides, and sometimes being divided amongst themselves. For example John of Menteith originally opposed Bruce but switched allegiance after Edward I of England, who supported the Balliol claim, died in 1308. The MacDonald family was also divided; Alexander Og MacDonald backed the Balliol claim and his brother, Angus Og, changed sides to support Robert the Bruce.

This period of turmoil allowed dispossessed families to try to regain lost property. One of these was Eoin MacSween who

Castle Sween (walk 24)

attempted to retake his ancestral seat at Castle Sween from the Stewart Earls of Menteith. On arrival, the MacSweens found an armed force in residence, and the castle remained part of the Menteith's holdings for another century or more. This episode is the subject of a famous Gaelic poem written in 1310 but it is an event that may have been fictitious.

With John of Menteith, the Campbells and Angus Og on his side in the west, Bruce was able to mount a campaign against the MacDougalls who supported the Balliol faction. After a siege of Dunstaffnage Castle, Alexander MacDougall was forced into exile in 1309. Thereafter the MacDougall lands were divided amongst the victors, Colin Campbell receiving the lands of Loch Awe and Ardskeadenish[3] (as the area around Kilmartin was known) in 1315. In 1326 Dugald Campbell (possibly Colin's brother) became sheriff of the newly established sheriffdom of Argyll. Angus Og MacDonald received his brother's lands, and in 1336 his son John MacDonald became the first Lord of the Isles to be officially recognised by the crown. His land was expanded through marriages; first to Amy MacRuari, who inherited her brother's estates

in north Argyll, and second to Margaret Stewart who had extensive lands in Kintyre.

Conflict resurfaced after the death of Robert I, which allowed Edward Balliol to make a bid for the throne, and he was backed by Edward III of England. The resurgence of the Balliol faction, particularly after Edward III's victory at Halidon Hill in 1333, threatened Menteith lands in the west, along with those of the Campbells, especially land that they had gained from dispossessed families. In 1329 David II of Scotland ascended the throne and an accommodation was tentatively reached with the ruling families in Argyll. By the end of the 14th century, the most important of these were the Clan Donald, who controlled the Hebrides, and the Clan Campbell in Argyll. The Lordship of the Isles, under the leadership of John of Islay, had never been fully consolidated in the eyes of the Crown and territorial disputes between families continued to occur. The support of the Church remained important, so it was patronised by the Lordship, the two institutions to some extent legitimising each other. Despite the multitude of conflicts, the Lordship of the Isles brought prosperity and a semblance of order to the west coast and islands. The swiftest method of transport was by sea, and the Lordship commanded a

---

[3]A variety of different spellings appear for this place name; we have chosen to reproduce the spelling used by Pont on a map of the 1590s.

fleet of birlinns (sailing galleys), fast moving ships which had much in common with earlier Viking longships.

The warrior culture prevalent in the area created Gaelic mercenaries who fought in both Scotland and Ireland. Those operating in Ireland came to be called Galloglass, a term that reflected their mixed Scottish and Norse roots. This was a militarised society and its unsettled nature, at least amongst the warring elites, is perhaps reflected in the fabulous and unique West Highland grave stones that can be seen throughout Argyll.

Images in Stone

The majority of carved gravestones date from the 13th to the 16th century and, as with other expressions of art during this time and in this place, blends Gaelic and Norse styles. From the 14th century Romanesque elements were added to create a unique West Highland style.

Many of the carved stones represent armed, helmeted knights. Swords and birlinns are also carved, along with hunting scenes, tools, fantastical beasts, and images of clergy. These are often surrounded by interlocking foliage and other embellishments. In common with histories of this period, women are rarely represented. Gravestones would have been laid flat on the grave. Later, stone tomb chests were sometimes used for burial; these were made of slabs – often carved – which sat above the ground. As well as gravestones, Argyll has some wonderfully elaborate carved crosses from this period, some known to have been erected by local dignitaries.

Researchers in the 1970s identified 'schools' of carved stones based on stylistic grounds. This has been re-examined recently and it is suggested that the different styles of carving are based on stylistic groupings rather than firm geographical locations. It seems likely that the stone carvers travelled within Argyll. For example many of the stones now on Iona are of a stone type that might have come from the quarries at Doide, near Kilmory Chapel. Rough-outs might have been produced at the quarry, and the carvings then completed where they were to be situated.

Antiquarians and museum curators in the early part of the 19th century were fascinated by the gravestones and carved crosses, and moved many of them to the National Museum of Scotland in Edinburgh and Kelvingrove Museum in Glasgow. Some have remained in the area however; Kilmartin Museum has a small display, and some stones from Kintyre can be seen in Campbeltown Museum. The two most extensive in situ collections in Mid Argyll are in Kilmartin and Kilmichael Glassary churchyards (walk 2 and walk 11) and there are others at Kilmory Chapel (walk 25), Keills (walk 23), Kilmarie (walk 4) and Kilberry.

As well as gravestones and crosses, relics would have been important. This is evidenced by the extraordinary discovery made at Torbhlaren Farm in the 19th century of an early 7th century bell encased within a highly decorated 12th century bell shrine. Bells were probably first used to call the community to worship but often became associated with a saint and were ascribed with a variety of semi-magical properties, including the ability to heal the sick. The bellshrine is elaborately decorated in the Hiberno-Norse style and can be seen, along with the bell itself, in the National Museum of Scotland.

The Lordship is Lost
The 15th century

Conflict between the MacDonald Lords of the Isles and the Scottish Crown continued into the 15th century, which saw a rising led by Donald, 2nd Lord of the Isles, who was defeated by the Regent Albany at the Battle of Harlaw in 1411. Thereafter Donald sought an accommodation with the Crown through peace talks at Lochgilphead, with the Campbells acting as mediators. The Campbells at this time were steadily expanding their influence in Argyll, for example, in 1427 Duncan Campbell exchanged the patrimony of his estate of Menstrie in Stirlingshire for Glassary.

Peace between the Crown and the Lords of the Isles was short lived. After an attempt by James I of Scotland to capture Alexander, 3rd Lord of the Isles, the MacDonalds (amongst others) rose up against the King but were defeated at Lochaber in 1429. Alexander's son John continued campaigning against the Crown but he was eventually to become an ally of the King in the 1430s.

The Campbells, on the other hand, were rewarded for backing the Crown. In 1457 Colin Campbell became Earl of Argyll and in 1471, Lord of Lorne. Aside from Kintyre, which was MacDonald land, the Campbell Earls controlled most of Argyll with the acquisition of this title. A branch of the family, known as the Campbells of Glenorchy (later the Earls of Breadalbane) had moved to control land to the north, from Loch Tay to Appin. Both branches of Campbells had relied more on astute marriages and the law courts than violence to assure their ascendancy.

Carved stone at Kilmory Oib (walk 20)

The death of James II in 1460 left a child King, James III, on the throne. John, 4th Lord of the Isles, sought to use this to his advantage. He was one signatory to the Treaty of Westminster - Ardtornish. Under this Pact he and others would become subjects of Edward IV of England and help him overthrow the Stewart dynasty. But the treaty between John and Edward IV came to light and recrimination was swift. Although John at first tried to resist, in 1476 he submitted to a sentence of forfeiture, losing some lands, but, crucially, keeping the Lord of the Isles title. Already bubbling family tensions were coming to the surface, however, and conflict between John and his illegitimate son Angus Óg soon broke out. In c1485, Angus Óg defeated his father in a naval battle. Although John remained head of the family, Angus Óg took power and set about trying to recover some of the territory his father had lost, but not long afterwards he was assassinated. His son, Donald Dubh, was captured and delivered to Innis Chonnel Castle on Loch Awe as a hostage to Colin Campbell, 1st Earl of Argyll. In the midst of the unrest James IV of Scotland, taking advantage of John's weak leadership, issued a second sentence of forfeiture in 1493. This required John to surrender his lands and titles to the Scottish Monarchy. The title is still held today by the male heir to the throne of the United Kingdom – currently His Royal Highness Prince Charles.

Having escaped incarceration and been recaptured, more than once, Donald Dubh, who had support from people in the Isles, made an alliance with England in an attempt to regain the MacDonald claim. But he died before he was able to act. Leadership of the 'Geadhealtacht' and thus political dominance of the area was bitterly fought over. As the MacDonald family fortunes fell those of the Campbells continued to rise during this period. They were granted land and strongholds, including Castle Sween, which they took possession of in 1481. The Campbells, like many other leading Highland families, straddled a cultural divide between Lowland and Highland Scotland, calling on both political prowess and military strength to retain power. Through political manoeuvring and clever marriages they steadily gained estates and power and closely aligned themselves with the Crown. Various branches of the Campbell family were responsible for castle building in Argyll. This includes Craignish Castle, likely to have been built in the early decades of the 15th century (walk 4). The earlier Duntrune Castle was also a Campbell stronghold at this time. For most of the

15th century Castle Sween had been in the possession of the MacDonald Lords of the Isles, placed in the hands of a constable, or keeper. One of these, Alexander MacMillan, ordered an elaborately carved cross to be erected to stand outside the Chapel at Kilmory Knap. This is now inside the chapel (walk 25). As well as the transfer of lands and castles to other prominent families, the demise of the Lordship brought to the fore inter-clan feuding once again, and a time known as the Linn nan Creach (The Era of Plundering and Chaos) ensued. Crannogs and duns might have been used during these turbulent times.

Buildings like Duntrune Castle and Castle Sween have left a very distinct mark of power and military strength on the Mid Argyll landscape – and we have a good deal of evidence about the lives of the people who ordered their construction. But of the lives of people of lesser status, we know little; only scant traces of medieval pottery have been found away from the major sites of occupation.

Turbulent Times Continue
The 16th century

Scotland was once again in turmoil at the beginning of the 16th century with the death of King James IV at the Battle of Flodden. He perished along with many others, including the Earl of Argyll. Another child King, James V, took the throne and Scotland was threatened by her aggressive southern neighbour, King Henry VII of England. Archibald Campbell, 4th Earl of Argyll, led a contingent of fighting men from the Highlands and Islands against Henry in support of the Scottish Regent Mary of Guise at the Battle of Pinkie in 1547. This century also marked the growing influence of the Protestant Church with the conversion of the gentry and their followers to the reformed faith. In 1558 the Catholic Archibald, Earl of Argyll, was succeeded by his son, also called Archibald, who became the 5th Earl, and who was a devout Protestant. New alliances were formed between prominent families – the MacDonalds, formerly bitter enemies of the Stewart dynasty, became their supporters. Conversely, the Campbells, who had supported the Catholic Stewarts, became their enemies. These shifting allegiances had far reaching consequences for both families and their supporters. The Earl remained a supporter of Mary Queen of Scots, and he was suspected of involvement in the murder of her husband Lord Darnley in 1567. Mary's increasing unpopularity led to a rebellion by her brother, the Earl of Moray, during which the Queen and her supporter, the Earl of Argyll, were defeated at Langside in 1568.

Castle building continued into the 16th century, either by the Campbells, or under their patronage. Kilmartin Castle (now a private residence) was built towards the end of the century, possibly erected by Neil Campbell, who was rector of Kilmartin from 1574 to 1627, and Bishop of Argyll between 1580 and 1608. One of the best preserved Castles in Kilmartin Glen is Carnassarie (walk 5), built between 1565 and 1572, probably on or near the foundations of older fortifications. Its construction was ordered by John Carswell, rector of Kilmartin, on land granted by the Earl of Argyll with whom he was very closely linked. Evidently ambitious and accomplished, by 1567 Carswell became Bishop of the Isles.

Bishop Carswell was a Gaelic speaker, and these linguistic skills were put to good use. He translated the Book of Common Order into Gaelic, which became the earliest printed book in Scots Gaelic – published in 1567. This book, written by John Knox, leader of the Reformation in Scotland, is a manual setting out how public worship should be conducted in the Reformed Church of Scotland. Himself a reformed minister, Carswell's translation would have been used all over the Gaelic speaking west coast, and it was also important in establishing standardised Gaelic spelling.

With the Reformation came the abrupt end of the by then centuries old tradition of West Highland grave slab carving.

The Early Modern Period
The 17th century to the 19th century

In the early years of the 17th century an event occurred that radically changed the course of Scottish history. The Union of the Crowns in 1603 saw James VI, King of Scots, inherit the English throne to become James I of England. In Argyll, the Campbells continued to rise, acquiring more holdings. In 1607 they were granted Kintyre, heartland of the MacDonalds, in gratitude for their suppression of the MacGregors, leaving the MacDonalds with no major land holdings in Scotland. While the Campbell power base in Argyll remained secure, their ascendancy was somewhat diminished by a series of family heads (all called Archibald) who were successively declared traitors for various infractions against the crown. The first of these, the 7th Earl, married Catholic Lady Anne Cornwallis and converted to her faith before going into exile. He joined the army of Phillip III of Spain, and was declared a traitor in 1619.

There was probably no love lost between old Archibald and his son the 8th Earl and later Marquess of Argyll, because the latter was a keen supporter of the Covenant, which he signed in 1638. The Covenanters were a Presbyterian movement and they eventually rose against King Charles I. The reasons for the covenanting wars, which were part of a civil war that affected England as well as Scotland, are very complex. The Earl's support of the Covenanters opened Argyll to retaliatory raids by Royalist forces led by the Duke of Montrose. In 1644 an army consisting mainly of Irish MacDonalds under Alistair MacColla joined Montrose in inflicting a crushing defeat on the Campbells at Inverlochy in 1646.

During this time, MacColla led brutal expeditions into Argyll and Campbell lands, in revenge for the loss of Kintyre. It is estimated that 18 parishes (including Glassary, Kilmartin and North Knapdale) were ravaged and that somewhere between 2,000 and 3,000 Campbells and their supporters were killed during these bloody times.

Unsurprisingly, many Campbell strongholds were garrisoned during this time, including Carnassarie and Duntrune Castles. One story is told that Duntrune Castle was warned by a piper of an imminent attack by MacColla's men who, being rather disgruntled, cut off both his hands. The ghost of the piper is said to still haunt Duntrune. Castle Sween was garrisoned and used as a supply base to distribute grain imported from Ireland. It is thought to have been captured and burned by Royalist forces in 1647, after which it fell into ruin. Older defensive structures were also refortified or became places of refuge.

MacColla's campaign came to an end when Charles I, having lost to Cromwell's armies, surrendered to the Scottish Covenanters. This freed up the main Scottish army under David Leslie to enter Argyll and pursue MacColla, who eventually fled. The Campbells, perhaps understandably, sought retaliation and set about punishing those who had joined MacColla. They led the forces that massacred the MacDonalds at Dunaverty. This and the slaughter of the Lamonts in Cowal are some of the atrocities committed at this time. Clans Campbell and Donald were however briefly united, fighting for King Charles I against Cromwell at the Battles of Dunbar and Worcester. Any gratitude owed by the Crown was soon forgotten, however; in 1661 the Marquess of Argyll was executed by Charles II for the part he played in the rebellion against his father Charles I. The Campbells lost the title of Marquess, but retained the earldom. On the death of Charles II his Catholic brother James II and VII succeeded. Evidently Archibald, the 9th Earl of Argyll, found this abhorrent for he joined a rather muddled rebellion led by the Duke of Monmouth, which ended in failure and the execution of Archibald in Edinburgh. The Earl's involvement in the rebellion sparked another invasion of Argyll by the Campbell's traditional enemies and, amongst other events, the siege and capitulation of Carnassarie Castle. Conflict between the Campbells and the Crown ended with the 10th Earl, who was rewarded with a Dukedom in 1689, partly for raising the first government sanctioned Highland regiment. He was also a prime mover of the 'Glorious Revolution' of 1688, where, shortly after, William of Orange and Mary, his wife, took the British crown.

Towards the end of the 17th century the country was largely at peace; however, there were more hard times to come. Failed harvests led to severe famine and economic depravation – and as always, the worst affected were the poor. Economic recovery into the 18th century was slow and some areas were left depopulated. In 1707 the Acts of Union united Scotland and England under one government as the two countries already shared a monarch. The Acts of Union were not welcomed by all in Scotland. The Campbells had recovered from the conflicts of the previous century and

become the dominant military and political force in the Highlands. They were used as a government bulwark against the Jacobite risings of 1715 and 1745 despite there being some Jacobite sympathisers in the clan Campbell diaspora.

Charles Edward Stewart (popularly known as Bonnie Prince Charlie) and his forces were crushed at the Battle of Culloden and the government exacted harsh recriminations after the 'Forty Five'. Partly because some Highland clans had assisted the rising, the government implemented wholesale destruction of the cultural, political and social system that underpinned them. Highland culture was suppressed – speaking Scottish Gaelic was forbidden, as was the wearing of Highland dress. Chiefs and Lairds were encouraged to develop their lands economically and so a cultural system that may well have been already in decline was destroyed. Highland culture was changed forever and the rural population suffered destitution and demoralisation.

The economic situation in Scotland began to improve in the middle of the 18th century. Cities emerged as centres of industry, commerce and trade and by the mid 18th century the Scottish Enlightenment was in full swing, securing the nation's place on the international stage. The Campbells continued their own building programmes, including the Seat of the Duke at Inveraray Castle – completed in 1760 to replace a 15th century tower house. The village was moved away from the castle at this time.

Changes came to Argyll in the form of roads and other infrastructure. One of these changes was the Crinan Canal (walk 13) – a 9 mile route for commercial sea going vessels between the Clyde and the west coast of Scotland that would avoid the risky waters around the Mull of Kintyre. Work began in 1794 and the Canal was fully completed in 1817. The building of the Canal had a profound impact on the area, in both social and economic terms. Over the years it took to build some workers would have been brought into the area. Locals would also have found employment – gruelling labour perhaps, but welcome money for most families. The village of Ardrishaig developed because of the Canal, as did other businesses along the route.

The Malcolm Family

In this new climate of economic prosperity fortunes were made and lost. The Campbell family was one to suffer financial misfortune in the 1790s, and they sold land to the Malcolms who were at that time in the ascendancy. The Malcolms, whose origins lay in the small MacCallum Clan, had become established in Mid Argyll as landowners in their own right by the middle of the 16th century and consolidated their position in the 17th century. Having become established in the Argyll colony in Jamaica by 1750, Dougald Malcolm, heir to the Poltalloch Estate, was a prosperous cattle rancher. Through marriage to a daughter of the Clerks of Braeleckan (also an Argyll family) he inherited a sugar plantation. It was at this time that the family name was anglicised from MacCallum to Malcolm. The family fortunes increased under Neill Malcolm who traded in commodities. The resulting prosperity of their estates abroad and at home was maintained through solid investments by Neill II and expanded under Neill III with substantial holdings in Australia. This self generated fortune enabled the Malcolms to increase their landholdings in Argyll, and they purchased estates from landowning families in financial difficulties. Land procured included the Duntrune and Raslie Estates, purchased from Neill Campbell in the 1790s, and the Dunardry Estate, acquired from the MacTavish family.

In the late 18th century George Malcolm began work on a new mansion house at one of the family's former places of residence. This building, known as Old Poltalloch, may never have been fully completed, although it is believed the farm steading was. In 1872 records describe Old Poltalloch as being in ruins, as George had become more involved in the family's interests in Jamaica. Neill I began the refurbishment of Duntrune Castle, a work that was continued by Neill II who also refurbished the original Kilmartin House, north of Kilmartin, after his purchase of that estate in the 1820s.

Neill I was one of the prime movers in the building of the Crinan Canal, and both Neill II and Neill III made substantial investments in roads and bridges in the area. Further improvements to the land were made by the drainage of the Mòine Mhór, begun by Neill I in 1794 and concluding under Neill III, by which time around 5,000 acres of ground had been reclaimed, of which 1,500 could be used as arable land. By the 1840s the estate had established slate quarries near the Crinan Canal and set up a tileworks (walk 8). The family also held lands and property in England.

Economic Development

Argyll's woodlands were important too in the industrialisation of Scotland during the 18th and 19th centuries. In Mid Argyll, woods were leased to the Bonawe Iron Furnace and were coppiced for the production of charcoal, used as fuel in the smelting process. Tree bark was used in the tanning industry, and other wood derived products were important. Fishing was a valuable industry; and the area was known for its export of livestock. From the 16th century there are records of cattle being driven to markets in the south, and by the beginning of the 18th century cattle droving had become a way of life, continuing well into the 19th century. There are many stances and piers dating to this period, and the Kilmichael Tryst (walk 11) – an annual cattle market and hiring fair – was an important social gathering. The Tryst ended with the coming of the railway to Oban, which reached the town in the 1880s.

The burgeoning tourist industry that flourished during the 19th century brought prosperity to the area. As a spin off from the Clyde paddle steamers taking holiday makers 'doon the watter', the Crinan Canal too had a paddle steamer – the Linnet, which took passengers along its length. As well as commercial sailing vessels from the 1870s, coal fired 'Clyde Puffers' used the route. These provided a vital supply link to the West Coast and Hebridean Islands.

Agriculture continued to be important throughout the early modern period in Argyll, but approaches began to change in the 1800s as new ideas were introduced. Improving farming methods were encouraged on the Poltalloch Estate during the 1800s, and particularly at the home farm at Barsloisnach (called Experiment at the time). Traditional land holding practices began to change all over Scotland at this time.

A common method of farming in Argyll had been the multiple, or joint, tenancy. In a similar, or simplified form, this may go back as far as the medieval period. Small clusters of domestic and farm buildings surrounded by arable land and grazing were held by the inhabitants as a group. Families shared the land – allotting use of the arable land, divided into strips, or rigs as they were known, annually. This ensured all families had a chance of being able to use the best land. Oats, barley and other crops were grown in the rigs. Generally tenants were obliged to have their grain ground in the estate

mill. Peat lands and grazing were held in common, and people were largely self sufficient. Cattle were the mainstay of the economy. During the summer, cattle would be taken to graze the hill pastures and people stayed in small stone and turf huts, known as sheilings, making cheese from the milk surplus.

All over Highland Scotland during the 18th and 19th centuries, people were displaced during agricultural reforms. In some areas people were expected to take up fishing, but many people chose to leave Scotland to seek a new life abroad, while others had little choice but to leave, since they had lost their homes. Although less brutally enacted than in other places, the process popularly known as the Highland Clearances, also affected Argyll. From Mid Argyll many people went to Canada or Australia, or to less

Kilmory village and chapel in 1870 (walk 25)

far flung places like Glasgow where work in the rapidly industrialising city was easier to find. One of the most notorious 'clearances' in Argyll occurred at Arichonan (walk 21). Tenants refused to comply with eviction orders made by the factor of the Poltalloch Estate, and a disturbance that threatened to spread into civil unrest took place. Eventually, the families left Arichonan, some departing for Canada. The process of rural depopulation, which continued into the middle of the 20th century, either through clearance or people leaving to seek a better life elsewhere, has left the Mid Argyll area with hundreds of now ruined settlements.

As rural settlements suffered depopulation, local towns began to develop and expand. Roy's map of 1750 shows a small settlement at Lochgilphead – the principal town in Mid Argyll. By 1801, it had grown considerably in size – partly developed by the Campbells and the MacNeills. By the 1860s the population had grown to over 1,600 people. Other buildings which played a role in some of the major events in the last few hundred years became derelict during this century. Carnassarie Castle was purchased by the Malcolms in 1829, and reported to be in ruins by 1844.

The Malcolm family under Neill III began what was to be their largest building project between 1849 and 1853; the construction of a new mansion at Callton Mór, also known as Poltalloch House. The cost of this Jacobean style mansion house was over £100,000. The house had vast policies encompassing much of Kilmartin Glen, as well as elaborate gates and gate houses. Many of the estate workers' cottages in the Glen, and Kilmartin Village itself, were built around the same time. By the mid 19th century, the old method of joint tenancy farming had been fully replaced by the improved system. This was characterised in Mid Argyll by consolidated land units and standardised farm houses. These farms had attached courtyard steadings, with ancillary buildings designed for a mixed farming system of dairy and beef cattle, with sheep on the higher ground. A typical example of this kind of farm is Balliemore (walk 11).

The Malcolm family built or rebuilt churches, and invested in their repairs. In 1854 they ordered the construction of the Episcopalian Chapel of St Columba on the Estate. Some carved crosses were moved to the grounds, probably to create a sense of antiquity. The past is something the family evidently had a continuing interest in, for some artefacts excavated from monuments in the Glen in the 1860s were displayed at Poltalloch House. One stone cross displayed at St Columba's Church was the Kilmichael Cross. This 14th or 15th century cross had originally stood as a memorial, or preaching cross, probably somewhere in Kilmichael Glen and became the market cross. Evidently, at some point it was removed because it was found (in two fragments) built into the fabric of an earlier Church that stood on the site of the existing Glassary Parish Church, which dates to 1873. The cross was repaired and erected at the newly built Episcopal Church. One hundred and fifty years of wind and rain weakened the repairs however. So, in 2009, it was conserved and repaired once again, and now stands in the grounds of Kilmartin Museum, having been loaned by the Trustees of St Columba's Episcopal Church. As part of the then fashionable interest in the past, the prehistoric remains in Kilmartin Glen became part of the designed landscape around Poltalloch House. The stone circles in the Glen were named Temple Wood and planted with oak trees. During this time the first antiquarian interest in Kilmartin Glen's prehistoric monuments resulted in some of the earliest excavations and it is a fascination that endures to this day.

Poltalloch Estate is now much smaller than it was at its height in the 19th century. Poltalloch House[4] was partially dismantled in 1957 and the Malcolm family home is once again Duntrune Castle.

Mid Argyll Today

At times Argyll has been at the forefront of nation changing events, at others, seemingly at the mercy of conflict, turmoil and bloodshed. Attempting to summarise 13,000 years of human history is a daunting task, but we hope that this brief introduction has given you a sense of the events and people who have shaped this very special place, and that through using this guide, you too will be able to see, experience and appreciate its magic.

[4]Please note that it is not possible to visit the ruins of Poltalloch House.

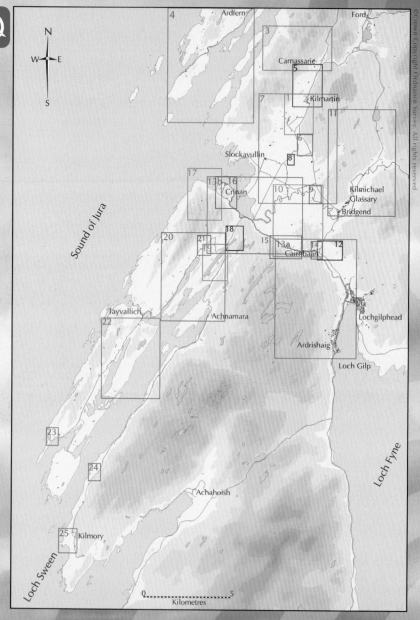

PART 2
THE WALKS

1 KILMARTIN GLEN PREHISTORIC MONUMENTS
KILMARTIN TO RI CRUIN

A remarkable concentration of prehistoric ritual and burial monuments including a stone circle and the linear cemetery, a line of five burial cairns stretching for over a mile down the Glen

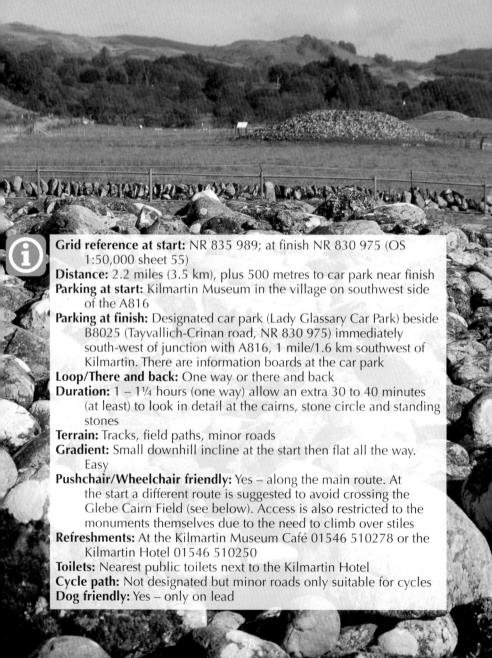

Grid reference at start: NR 835 989; at finish NR 830 975 (OS 1:50,000 sheet 55)

Distance: 2.2 miles (3.5 km), plus 500 metres to car park near finish

Parking at start: Kilmartin Museum in the village on southwest side of the A816

Parking at finish: Designated car park (Lady Glassary Car Park) beside B8025 (Tayvallich-Crinan road, NR 830 975) immediately south-west of junction with A816, 1 mile/1.6 km southwest of Kilmartin. There are information boards at the car park

Loop/There and back: One way or there and back

Duration: 1 – 1¼ hours (one way) allow an extra 30 to 40 minutes (at least) to look in detail at the cairns, stone circle and standing stones

Terrain: Tracks, field paths, minor roads

Gradient: Small downhill incline at the start then flat all the way. Easy

Pushchair/Wheelchair friendly: Yes – along the main route. At the start a different route is suggested to avoid crossing the Glebe Cairn Field (see below). Access is also restricted to the monuments themselves due to the need to climb over stiles

Refreshments: At the Kilmartin Museum Café 01546 510278 or the Kilmartin Hotel 01546 510250

Toilets: Nearest public toilets next to the Kilmartin Hotel

Cycle path: Not designated but minor roads only suitable for cycles

Dog friendly: Yes – only on lead

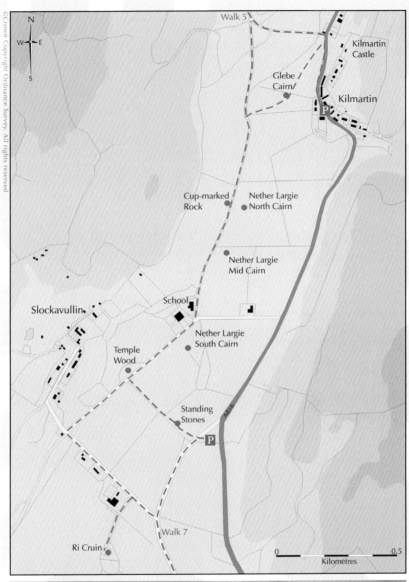

Walk 5

Kilmartin Castle

Glebe Cairn

Kilmartin

Cup-marked Rock

Nether Largie North Cairn

Nether Largie Mid Cairn

Slockavullin

School

Nether Largie South Cairn

Temple Wood

Standing Stones

A816

Walk 7

Ri Cruin

0   Kilometres   0.5

From Kilmartin Museum car park entrance, turn left along the roadside path, as indicated by a signpost to Carnassarie and Dunadd. Before the Kilmartin Garage there is a kissing gate to the field; go through the gate and cross the field to get to the Glebe Cairn.

Wheelchairs and pushchair users can, instead, pass Kilmartin Garage and take the minor road to the left. At the top of this road turn left onto 'The Coach Road' which is signposted Dunadd. Within 200 metres you will reach the footbridge over the Kilmartin Burn as detailed below.

From the Glebe Cairn head towards the footbridge over the Kilmartin Burn. Cross the bridge and turn left onto a track, called 'The Coach Road.'

Glebe Cairn

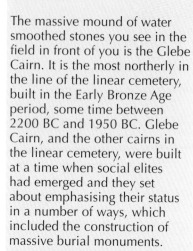

The massive mound of water smoothed stones you see in the field in front of you is the Glebe Cairn. It is the most northerly in the line of the linear cemetery, built in the Early Bronze Age period, some time between 2200 BC and 1950 BC. Glebe Cairn, and the other cairns in the linear cemetery, were built at a time when social elites had emerged and they set about emphasising their status in a number of ways, which included the construction of massive burial monuments.

The Glebe Cairn was partially excavated in 1864 by Reverend Greenwell, a Canon from Durham Cathedral. Greenwell's work revealed various phases of use and

Glebe Cairn, Kilmartin Museum and Church

reuse, which is typical of most of the prehistoric monuments in the Glen. His report is one of the earliest entries in the 'Proceedings of the Society of Antiquaries of Scotland' volumes, a publication that continues today.

Greenwell's work determined that the first burial on the site was placed in a cist, around which two concentric rings of stones had been constructed. The cist was found to contain an incomplete jet necklace made up of beads and spacer plates, as well as one of the finest pottery vessels in Scotland – an Irish style Food Vessel. This style of pottery is thought to have held offerings of food for the dead, perhaps to sustain them for the journey to the Otherworld.

Necklaces of this kind are rare finds. The nearest source of jet is in Yorkshire, so this object would have been brought over some distance, which tells us that the person who owned it was of high status. Recent research has shown that these objects were sometimes worn for generations, before being interred as grave goods. They are generally found in the graves of females, and so although Greenwell found no human remains (they had probably completely decomposed) the grave was most likely that of an important woman or girl.

The grave was later incorporated into a larger round cairn, the focus of which was a secondary cist built in its centre. This cist also contained a highly decorated Food Vessel; again it had stylistic links to Ireland. Both vessels can be seen on display in Kilmartin Museum where they are on loan from the National Museum of Scotland and the British Museum. The necklace, along with a number of other prehistoric objects, had been displayed at the now ruined Poltalloch House, but sadly they were lost in a fire.

Food Vessel from Glebe Cairn

This is the point at which wheelchair and pushchair users rejoin the walk.

Continue on the Coach Road until you reach a stile over the fence on your left, where you will reach the Nether Largie North Cairn, the next in the linear cemetery.

Nether Largie North Cairn

This cairn is another massive burial monument similar to the Glebe Cairn. After excavation by James Hewat Craw in 1930, the cairn was completely rebuilt and heavily modified so that visitors can now go inside, but this would not have been possible in prehistory.

Under the water smoothed stones that make up the cairn material, Craw discovered, slightly off centre, a massive cist, which had been dug into the natural ground surface. The top slab of the cist had been covered with a number of other stone slabs. When opened, the underside of the cist's top slab was found to have been decorated with at least forty cup marks and around ten carvings in the shape of flat axeheads. The end slab has also been carved with the shape of two flat axes. You can see both these carved slabs inside. Axeheads at this time would have been made of copper or bronze, and are some of the first metal objects used at this time. The use of the axehead as a motif is later than the cup markings, so it is possible that this slab was originally a cup marked slab that was then moved and reshaped as a cist slab, and the axehead carvings added. Look out for the axehead carvings which overlie cup marks, an obvious indication of respective chronology. Whoever had been buried in this ostentatious grave was a person of great importance. But their remains had long since decomposed when Craw opened the cist, for all that remained was a single tooth, some charcoal and ochre. Ochre is an earth based pigment which produces a reddish colour and probably had a symbolic significance.

An oval pit had been dug about three metres from this

Carvings inside Nether Largie North Cairn

burial, in which Craw found an ox tooth and more fragments of charcoal. This might have been a grave, or the remains of a pit dug for a funerary feast.

A setting of stones, including two upright slabs, was found close to the cist during the excavation, but its purpose remains unclear. One of the upright stones is carved with the shape of two circles, and like the cist slab, might have been part of an earlier monument which was then incorporated into Nether Largie North Cairn. This stone is now on display at Kilmartin Museum, having been kindly lent by the National Museum of Scotland.

 As you go back to the main path, look over the fence (but please don't climb over it) opposite the stile and see if you can spot a small exposure of a cup marked slab in the grass.

Back on the main path, walk along until you reach the stile, then a fenced path leading to Nether Largie Mid Cairn.

Nether Largie Mid Cairn

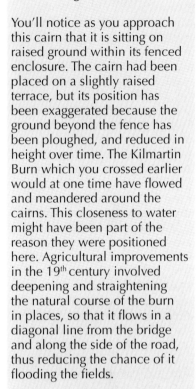

You'll notice as you approach this cairn that it is sitting on raised ground within its fenced enclosure. The cairn had been placed on a slightly raised terrace, but its position has been exaggerated because the ground beyond the fence has been ploughed, and reduced in height over time. The Kilmartin Burn which you crossed earlier would at one time have flowed and meandered around the cairns. This closeness to water might have been part of the reason they were positioned here. Agricultural improvements in the 19th century involved deepening and straightening the natural course of the burn in places, so that it flows in a diagonal line from the bridge and along the side of the road, thus reducing the chance of it flooding the fields.

Nether Largie Mid Cairn was constructed around the same time as the Glebe Cairn and Nether Largie North, but it appears much smaller now. Indeed it was reported to have

Nether Largie Mid Cairn

stood around 3 metres high in the 1920s, but was greatly reduced by the end of this decade when it was excavated by Craw in 1929, the stones having been removed for road repairs.

Under the stones, Craw found a cist which had been built in a pit dug into the natural ground surface. Its position is now indicated by concrete posts. A second cist was found, and this is now visible at the southern end. The top slab has been propped open so that you can see inside. The side slabs have been grooved so that the end slabs could be fitted into them, a technique more usually used with wood. Look out for a cup mark and a carving of a flat axehead on the inner surface of the northwest end slab. By the time Craw opened the cists, both were empty, all the original contents having decomposed.

Another cup marked stone can be seen about 10 metres to the north east from the open cist.

You can also see traces of the kerb stones that once surrounded the edge of the cairn.

Resuming the main line of the walk, you'll soon come to a minor intersection where Kilmartin Primary School is on the right. The fields to your left are thought to be the location of a sixth cairn in the linear cemetery (there is no visible evidence remaining). Continue towards Dunadd (as signposted) straight ahead along the minor road to a gate on the left. From here there is a short path to Nether Largie South Cairn.

Nether Largie South Cairn

You have reached Nether Largie South Cairn, the oldest in the Linear Cemetery, and one of the oldest monuments in the Glen.

Nether Largie South Cairn

Greenwell excavated this site in 1864 when he found what we now call a megalithic chamber tomb of a style known as a Clyde Cairn. Unlike the other cairns you have seen, Nether Largie South was originally designed so that the living could also enter. It was a place of burial for generations before being modified to make it look more like the Early Bronze Age cairns in the linear cemetery, which took this site as the basis for their alignment. The remodelling and incorporation of this older monument might have been an act of reverence to the ancestors perhaps, but the appropriation of this monument was also a way of latching onto the memory, and thus the power and prestige, of past inhabitants of the Glen.

The first phase of monument building at Nether Largie South began in the early Neolithic period, about 3700 – 3600 BC. A chamber nearly 6 metres long was built, divided into four segments by large slabs and interspersed with stretches of dry stone walling. Two large portal stones were placed at the entrance, which may have originally been more elaborate, with a curving façade, but this cannot be confirmed since it is now covered in water smoothed stones.

The mound covering the inner chamber might have stood some four metres high, and it would originally have been rectangular or trapezoid in shape. Greenwell discovered that people had been buried here, but we do not know the whereabouts of these human remains now. A Neolithic pottery vessel dating to 3600 – 3500 BC, which he also found, is now on display in Kilmartin Museum, on loan from the British Museum.

Greenwell found much evidence, albeit somewhat disturbed, of later use from the Chalcolithic Period, dating between 2300 BC and 2000 BC. A small cist had been built inside the chamber and this contained a Beaker pot. Cremated human remains and sherds of another Beaker pot, along with barbed and tanged flint arrowheads and smashed quartz pebbles, were found in the chamber. Slightly later, two cists dating between 2200 BC and 1900 BC were dug into the outer cairn material. These cists might be part of the Early Bronze Age modifications that changed the shape of the monument to match that of the other cairns. On the south side of the outside of Nether Largie South Cairn you can still see one of these cists.

Return to the minor road and continue along the road to the stone wall enclosing Temple Wood. Enter through a low gate to visit the North East and South West Stone Circles. There is disabled parking directly adjoining Temple Wood.

Temple Wood

Temple Wood

The enclosure and oak trees around the site date to the 19th century, as does the name Temple Wood. The site was also called Half Moon Wood at this time. In the 19th century, there was a romantic interest in ancient druids. Some believed stone circles were temples of the druids; however the 'druids' as described by Roman writers belong to a time thousands of years later, so had no connection to stone circles at all.

When building began on this site, Nether Largie South Chambered Cairn had probably been standing for at least 500 years. You will see that there are two circles,

although the one to the north east is now represented by a circular spread of water rolled stones and concrete pads. This was only revealed during excavation work undertaken by Jack Scott in the 1970s. The site had been partially excavated in 1929. However, Scott's detailed work, and more recent radio carbon dating work organised by the National Museum of Scotland, has revealed so much about the complicated history of use and reuse at this site, which spanned at least two thousand years. But, of course, the story doesn't end there for the site remains special to many people today.

The first phase of activity began around 3000 BC to 2900 BC during the late Neolithic period, when people erected a timber circle on the North East site. This was followed by the erection of a stone circle in the same spot. Probably soon after, the focus moved to the South West, and a stone circle (actually an ovoid shape) was erected. The two circles were perhaps in use at the same time. Two of the stones at the South West circle have designs pecked onto their surface, concentric circles on one, and the other represents a spiral with strong links to Irish passage grave art of the same period. This spiral is still faintly visible, snaking around two adjacent surfaces of the upright stone to the north of the circle.

Although the use of stone circles has been debated at length, and will probably continue to be, it is generally accepted that they were places of ceremony, where rites and rituals might have been performed – a place where a sense of community was reinforced through the activities which occurred there. These rites and rituals may well have involved the marking of celestial events, and it has been argued that Temple Wood has both solar and lunar alignments.

Later, however, between 2300 BC and 2000 BC, the focus of the site turned to burial and two cist graves with small cairns were constructed

Spiral carvings at Temple Wood

outside the circle. One of these cists contained a Beaker and three barbed and tanged arrowheads, all of which are now on display in Kelvingrove Museum in Glasgow.

Later still, in the centre of the South West circle a massive cist was constructed, and a ring of stones (known as a ring cairn) was built by filling in the gaps between the standing stones and the addition of water rolled stones outside. This ring cairn covered the small cairns outside the circle. It has been suggested that the spiral design on one of the upright stones might have been extended to another face of the stone at this time so that it might not be totally obscured by the ring cairn.

It might have been around this time that stones from the North East circle were removed, some possibly reused in monuments elsewhere in the Glen.

Then around 1450 BC and 1200 BC, in what was now the centre of the ring cairn, people built two kerb cairns, which contained cremated human remains. One was used twice. Both these cairns have what archaeologists call 'false portals' which face south east – hinting at an astronomical alignment.

Having been the focus of ritual activity for 2,000 or so years, around 1000 BC, when peat had probably began to form in the Glen and around the site, Temple Wood ceased to be a focus for prehistoric people. The upright stones would have been visible for perhaps thousands of years as is shown in William Daniell's engraving of 1813, which illustrates peat cutting taking place close to the stones.

Evidently the stones were seen as a resource too, for one has been partially reshaped to make a mill stone – work that was never completed and so the stone was never removed.

Following Jack Scott's extensive excavations, the site was reconstructed with a view to receiving visitors – showing as many of the features as possible, but in prehistory, Temple Wood would never have looked as it does today.

If you wish to finish the walk here, you can follow the path from almost opposite Temple Wood, across a field (which contains the Nether Largie Standing stones) to the Lady Glassary Wood car park at the finishing point of this walk (see above).

Nether Largie Standing Stones

(Sometimes called Lady Glassary Standing Stones after the nearby Lady Glassary Wood, and also known as stone rows).

This impressive and complex setting of stones consists of four groups of stones aligned roughly north east and south west and originally had two outliers – only one of which now remains. Aside from the outlying stone, you will see two pairs of standing stones with two larger groups in between. One of these stones stands

Nether Largie Standing Stones

nearly 3 metres high, and bears a complex series of cup and ring markings. Two other stones (one in each group of two) bear rock art.

Survey work has detected other features in the fields around the stones and a cist was found nearby.

It has been suggested that this setting of stones might be contemporary with the Ballymeanoch Stones (walk 6) which date to the Middle Bronze Age, between 1400 BC and 1050 BC. There are obvious similarities in layout, and both groups of stones have rock carvings, although the Nether Largie Stones are a more complex layout. If the dating is accurate, these stones were built around 500 years after the Early Bronze Age linear cemetery, and at least 1,500 years after the stone circles at Temple Wood were constructed.

As with Ballymeanoch, it has been suggested that these stones were erected to mark lunar events, although others have argued that both lunar and solar events were marked here at Nether Largie.

To reach the last site on this walk, from Temple Wood continue along the minor road to a T-junction. Slockavullin is signposted to the right.

Cist Cemetery

The huge cairns erected in the Glen were the burial places of the elite. People of lesser status were interred in more modest graves – which took the form of burial cists, sometimes grouped together to form cist cemeteries.

There are numerous cists in the glen and there is one such cist cemetery behind the gate lodge[1] of the now ruined Poltalloch House. The site was investigated and the remains of both adults and children were found, along with grave goods including pottery and flint knives. One of the cists contained another jet and cannel coal necklace made up of spacer plates and beads, together with a bracelet made of cannel coal beads which is on display in the National Museum of Scotland in Edinburgh. This find indicates that not everyone who was important enough to have been buried with a necklace was buried under a massive cairn.

Turn left along the minor road and continue until you reach the signposted turnoff to Ri Cruin. Cross a stone stile, follow the grassy path between fields, and cross a small burn to reach the cairn, surrounded by well spaced trees.

[1]This site is not accessible to the public.

Ri Cruin

Today this is the most southerly cairn in the Early Bronze Age linear cemetery. Local tradition has it that it is the burial place of a king. Although our understanding of the concept of Kingship might not have resonated with the cairn's prehistoric builders, Ri Cruin was certainly built to express social status and the importance of the people interred there.

Built 4,000 years ago, between 2200 BC and 1950 BC, it had been used in more recent times as the site of a lime kiln, and so many of the water rolled stones that would have made up the cairn have been removed, some of the deposits disturbed, and it is much reduced in size. Excavations have taken place here on three occasions, firstly by Reverend Mapleton, an Episcopalian Dean of Argyll, in 1870, then Craw in 1929, and again by the well known archaeologist V. Gordon Childe in 1936. The site was then reconstructed with a view to its being visited by the public and all traces of the lime kiln were removed.

Three cists were found but only two are now visible. The most northerly had been set into a pit and the side slabs had been carved with grooves so that the end slabs could fit snugly against them. Cremated human bones were found inside. This cist had previously been opened, so any grave goods placed with the cremated remains might have been removed.

A second cist was erected to the south east, inside the kerb stones that edged the cairn, which also had grooved side slabs. Nothing was found inside and the cist itself had been removed by the time Craw investigated the site.

A third cist was constructed just outside the southern end of the cairn. Its cap slab is sitting to one side of the cist so that you can see inside. This was also empty of any grave goods or human remains. Two of the stones that make up the cist have been carved. One – an end slab – remains on the site, and can be seen. It has been carved with representations of seven flat axeheads on its inner surface. The other carved stone was removed and taken to Poltalloch House[2], where it was lost in the same fire which destroyed the necklace from the Glebe Cairn. A cast of the stone had been made previously, however, and this survives in the National Museum of Scotland collections. Recent research indicates that this stone had a complex history.

[2]Please note that it is not possible to visit the ruins of Poltalloch House as it is now in a very dangerous state.

It might originally have belonged to an earlier Neolithic monument dating to around 2900 BC, and then been reused in the cist some time between 2200 BC and 1950 BC. At this time the carving might have been added to make it look more like a halberd – a metal tipped weapon.

Traces of kerb stones that would have surrounded the cairn can still be seen within the cairn material.

Carvings at Ri Cruin

To reach the end of this walk, return to the minor road and turn right, then at the T junction turn left along the B8025; Lady Glassary Wood car park is about 400 metres further on the right. To continue to Dunadd (walk 7) turn right at the T junction.

The best collection of West Highland carved slabs in Scotland

Grid reference: at start and finish NR 835 989 (OS 1:50,000 sheet 55)

Distance: 45 metres

Parking: at start and finish Kilmartin Museum (NR 835 989) or in the village on southwest side of the A816

Loop/There and back: There and back

Duration: 30 minutes

Terrain: Stony paths

Gradient: Flat other than the graveyard which extends down the slope

Pushchair/Wheelchair friendly: Yes with the exception of the Poltalloch enclosure and the Lapidarium

Refreshments: At the Kilmartin Museum Café 01546 510278 or the Kilmartin Hotel 01546 510250

Toilets: Nearest public toilets next to the Kilmartin Hotel

Cycle path: No

Dog friendly: On a lead only

From the Museum car park either walk to the entrance, turn right for 45 metres along the pavement then right through the gates to the churchyard. Alternatively enter the churchyard via the door in the wall on the south side of the car park.

The Church History

The 'Kil' element in the place name indicates an ecclesiastical presence on the site since the 8th or 9th century – borne out by the early dates of some of the carved crosses found here. Written records describe a Church building of 1601, which might have incorporated parts of an earlier, medieval building.

The Church of 1601 was replaced in 1798, and this building was itself replaced by the present Church, built in 1834–5. A slab carved with the date 1798 lies in the churchyard, a relic of the earlier building.

The manse where the minister lived and the associated farm buildings were built in 1789. These now house Kilmartin Museum, shop and café and are accessible from the churchyard via a door in the wall.

In Kilmartin churchyard

Kilmartin Church from the air

The Poltalloch Enclosure

The burial enclosure of the Malcolms of Poltalloch is to the south side of the Church. You can view the gravestones from a wooden platform. Some are medieval (14th to 15th century) but were reused for later interments and inscriptions were added at this time.

The Churchyard

Originally the churchyard extended along the flat gravel terrace, but pressure for space resulted in an extension down the slope between 1883 and 1887.

The Poltalloch Enclosure

The Church Interior

Inside the Church, towards the rear of the building, are three crosses – brought inside for protection. The cross carved with interlocking key patterns and spirals is thought to date from the 9th or 10th century AD.

The Lapidarium

The Lapidarium (place where stones are displayed) was formerly a Mausoleum of 17th century date. It was rebuilt in the 1950s to protect the stones, all of which would originally have stood outside.

Most of the stones here are of medieval date, ranging from the 13th to 15th century. As you enter, the earliest are on the left side, the later ones on the right. These are grave slabs which would originally have been laid flat over a grave.

The one exception is the side of a chest tomb – a grave made up of four side slabs and one top slab – raised above the ground rather than sunk into it.

The stones at Kilmartin are the best collection of West Highland grave slabs in Scotland. Most are of a style we call the 'Loch Awe School', which tended towards designs representing armoured men, swords and spears. You can also see fantastical beasts and interlaced foliage patterns.

Grave slab in the Lapidarium

3 ORMAIG FROM CARNASSARIE CAR PARK

An internationally important rock art site

Grid reference at start and finish: NM 839 004 (OS 1:50,000 sheet 55)
Distance: 4.4 miles/7 km
Parking at start and finish: Carnassarie Castle car park adjacent to
  west side of A816, 1 mile/1.6 km northeast of Kilmartin
Loop/There and back: There and back
Duration: 2 – 2¼ hours walking; 30 minutes to look at rock art
Terrain: Farm and forest tracks, muddy in places; narrow, rough path
Gradient: Steady ascent then descent both out and back. Strenuous
Pushchair/Wheelchair friendly: No
Refreshments: At the Kilmartin Museum Café 01546 510278 or the
  Kilmartin Hotel 01546 510250
Toilets: Nearest public toilets next to the Kilmartin Hotel
Cycle path: Yes to Information Board
Dog friendly: On a lead only

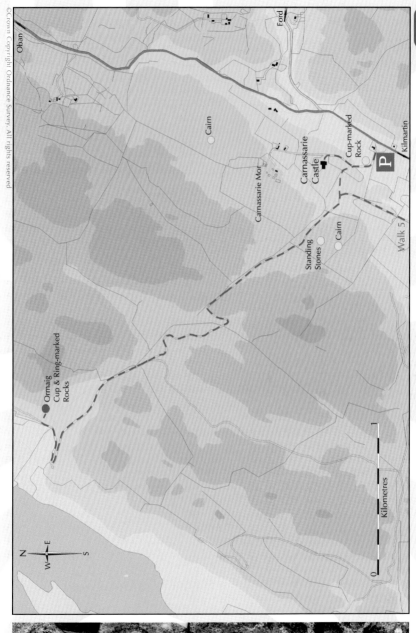

Oban

Ford

Kilmartin

Cairn

Carnassarie Mor

Carnassarie Castle

Cup-marked Rock

Walk 5

Standing Stones

Cairn

Ormaig Cup & Ring-marked Rocks

Kilometres

N
W E
S

Standing stones at Carnassarie

Before you set out, check the information boards at the car park. Go through a stone 'squeeze stile' gate in the top right corner of the car park to a vehicle track; note the black-banded waymarker post used along this walk. The track gains some height and imposing Carnassarie Castle comes into view – at first glance you might think it's still occupied. Continue uphill; just 25m short of the entrance to the castle grounds is a track junction where you turn left for Ormaig (signed Kilmartin). For more information about the castle see walk 5.

Go up, through a gate, and left along a farm track. It dog-legs around the edge of the field to a junction where you would turn left for Kilmartin and right for Ormaig, as indicated by a waymarker. The grassy track rises through the wide glen; on the left as you start to walk up, after approximately 200 - 300 metres, there are two standing stones and the remains of a burial cairn. The burial cairn was excavated in 1930 and at that time was probably already much smaller than it had been in prehistory. Close to the centre of the cairn was a cist, which contained a pottery vessel, charcoal and some ochre (pigment). This spot affords a very good view of Kilmartin Glen.

Make your way back to the path, pass through a gate and continue on the track, which can be soft after rain, to the top of the hill.

On the trail to Ormaig

Almost immediately, you go into ground used for commercial forestry. The current forest track, which follows the line of an old road built by the Poltalloch Estate in the 19th century, descends, winds round a side glen and traverses through more ground used for commercial forestry. You will then turn right to join a wide forest track, which soon descends, opening up to a fine view north westwards across Loch Craignish to the yachts clustered in Ardfern Harbour. The track goes down through a steep-sided glen to a junction where there's a derelict stone cottage on the left. Take a sharp right hand turn and descend to a burn. On the right, set back from the track, there is an information board about Ormaig.

Follow the narrow path up beside the burn; within 150 metres it diverges left then bends sharply to traverse the edge of the slope for about 100 metres to an open grassy knoll where you'll find the decorated rock surface.

Ormaig photographed at night

The Ormaig rock art site is one of the best in Europe. Carved perhaps 4 or 5,000 years ago, this site was rediscovered in 1974 by forestry workers who were planting the hillside of what was formerly Ormaig Farm with spruce trees. The site had been known in the 1800s as is evidenced by the names carved into the rock surfaces by John Campbell in 1874 and Archie Campbell in 1877. The site is now a Scheduled Ancient Monument and protected from further additions to the carvings by law. Between the 1800s and the 1970s the site became covered with vegetation and slipped out of memory.

When it was rediscovered the full extent of the site was not known. The area around the site was planted, and the site became a clearing in a dense forest plantation. Recently this was felled and the outlook now looks perhaps more like it did in prehistory with views across the water to the Craignish Peninsula.

In advance of tree felling, Kilmartin Museum, assisted by staff and students from the University of Southampton, undertook a small excavation which aimed to determine the size of the outcrops, and to see if there were traces of other activity at the site. Two more, previously unrecorded, panels of rock art were found and the first plan showing the panels in relation to each other was produced. Scant traces of worked stone were also found. It is likely that there may have been traces of other prehistoric activity here, but these are undetectable now following tree planting.

There are seven discrete panels (or exposures) of rock art at the site. Look out for the distinctive 'rosettes' (exposure 1 south), and the parallel lines of grooves (exposure 2). Part of the earthfast surface of one panel was broken off by tree root action and is now in the safekeeping of Kilmartin Museum.

Why is Ormaig rock art here? It is difficult to answer this question but it is possible that the position of the sea in relation to the site of this very complex panel would have been significant. It might have marked the position of an easy passage over the hills down into Kilmartin Glen with its extensive complex of ritual and burial monuments.

Cup marks, rings and grooves on exposure 2 at Ormaig

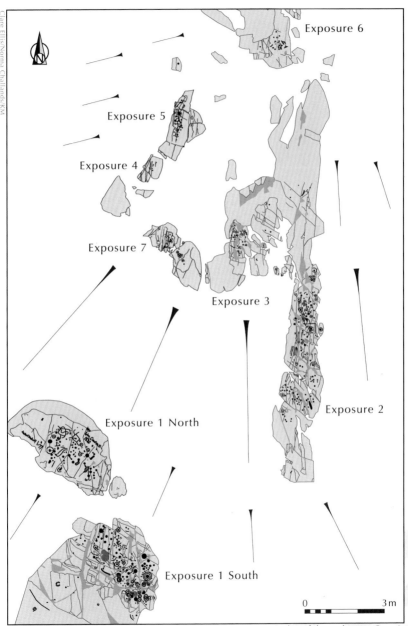

Clare Ellis/Norma Challands/KM

Exposure 6

Exposure 5

Exposure 4

Exposure 7

Exposure 3

Exposure 1 North

Exposure 2

Exposure 1 South

0   3 m

A plan of the rock art at Ormaig

The return journey is simply a matter of retracing your steps.

4 ARDFERN AND CRAIGNISH

OLD PARISH CHURCH, KILMARIE CHAPEL AND CARVED STONES

Ruined chapel and many medieval carved stones as well as wonderful sea views

Grid reference at start and finish: NM 778 015 (OS 1:50,000 sheet 55)

Distance: 150 metres to the Chapel from the car park or 5 miles/8 km from village to Chapel

Parking at start and finish: Either an informal roadside parking area on the left of the B8002, just short of the signposted access road to Craignish Castle (NM 778 015) or in Ardfern village (NM 805 043).

Loop/There and back: There and back

Duration: 10 – 12 minutes or 3 – 3¼ hours (depending on choice of walk)

Terrain: Road (optional), shore line, vehicle track, grass

Gradient: Negligible. Easy

Pushchair/Wheelchair friendly: Yes (although the hill just before the Chapel is steep and the graveyard is grass)

Refreshments: At the Galley of Lorne Inn 01852 500284 or the Crafty Kitchen Tea Room 01852 500303, both in Ardfern village

Toilets: No public toilets in Ardfern

Cycle path: Yes

Dog friendly: Yes – although on lead only on the road sections

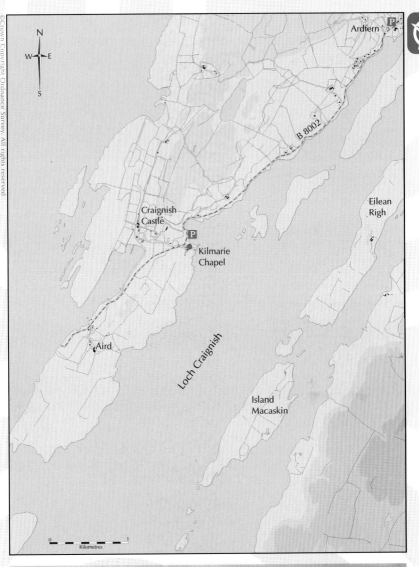

Ardfern

B 8002

Eilean Righ

Craignish Castle

Kilmarie Chapel

Aird

Loch Craignish

Island Macaskin

Kilometres

The coast near Ardfern

If you have parked in Ardfern village head along the road, past the Crafty Kitchen Tea Room and Galley of Lorne Inn (dating to around 1700). Continue on past the Parish Church. The present building dates to 1827, and replaced a building of 1740, which itself had replaced a church of 1698.

Walk along the quiet, scenic road beside Loch Craignish to the Chapel, a distance of 5 miles/8 km return. Long stretches of this walk can be done along the shoreline of Loch Craignish.

From the minor road go through a gateway on the left, past the modern graveyard to the entrance to the older burial ground where there is a sign for 'Craignish Sculptured Stones'. The stones are housed in the Chapel, partially roofed for their protection. The entrance is in the south wall.

The ruined Church, which once served as the parish Church of Craignish, is medieval in date. The roof has been partially rebuilt to shelter some of the very fine carved stones from the site. Kilmarie (Kilvaree) is dedicated to St Maelrubha of Applecross, an Irish Monk who lived in the 7th century. It is thought that he travelled in the area before establishing a monastery at Applecross in Wester Ross.

The Church building itself dates from the 13th century, although later modifications and repairs can be detected. There may have been an earlier Church at the site as is evidenced by the 'kil' element in the place name.

The entrance is in the south wall. Note the original inner door jambs, and the later medieval modifications to the

Loch Craignish

outer part of the doorway.
Look out also for the aumbries
(recesses or cupboards used to
store chalices and other objects
used in services) towards the
ends of the east wall and in the
south wall.

There are information signs
which give more detail on the
chapel and the stones, 17 of
which were brought under
cover in the 1970s for their
protection, but which would
have originally been in the
graveyard. The gravestones
mostly date to the 14th and
15th centuries and are carved
from local stone, including
epidiorite, although some are
slate from Easdale. The carvings
depict weapons, warriors and
other figures. Look out for the
two 10th century crosses. The
date of these carvings suggests
there may have been an earlier
building here.

Near Craignish Castle

There is a stone socket for
a standing cross, which has a
Sundial carved on one corner.
Inside the main space of the
chapel you will see some 16th
century chest tombs in which
important people were buried.
One has been carved with a
hunting scene.

This chapel remains a place
of worship and burial so please
be respectful of this.

There are also more stones
in the graveyard, and from the
south western boundary you
can see the ruins of Kirkton
township.

To return to the village retrace
your steps along the road or
shoreline. Alternatively the walk
can be extended by turning left
on the road towards Craignish
Castle and the Sound of Jura.
Once back on the road, continue
to the first fork in the road. Take
the left hand fork and continue
for a further 1.5 miles to the end
of the road. The road ends at a
pier from which cattle used to be
swum to Jura. This section of road
walking is very pleasant – you
can see Craignish Castle, much
extended and altered from its
origin as a late medieval tower
house. The Castle is inhabited
and not open to the public. Along
the way there are many waders
and seabirds to be seen, and from
the grassy knoll adjoining the
pier you might be able to spot
the churning waters of the world
famous Corryvreckan whirlpool.

CARNASSARIE CASTLE

A fine, well-preserved 16th century tower house

Grid reference at start and finish: NM 839 004 (OS 1:50,000 sheet 55)
Distance: 1 mile/1.6 km plus optional extension
Parking at start and finish: In Carnassarie Castle car park adjacent to west side of A816
Loop/There and back: There and back
Duration: 1 hour
Terrain: Tracks
Gradient: Gradual ascent (height gain about 50m). Moderate
Pushchair/Wheelchair friendly: No
Refreshments: At the Kilmartin Museum Café 01546 510278 or the Kilmartin Hotel 01546 510250
Toilets: Nearest public toilets next to the Kilmartin Hotel
Cycle path: Yes until the steps which lead up to the Castle
Dog friendly: Under close control only

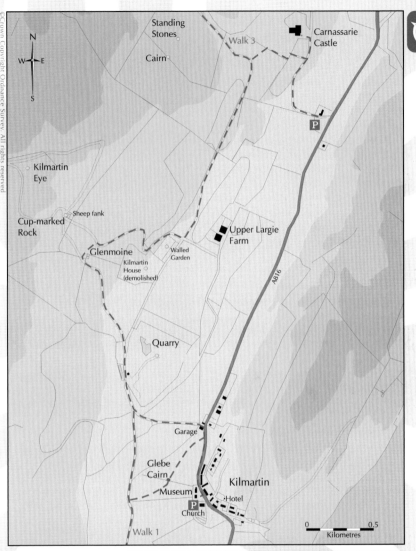

N
W — E
S

Standing
Stones

Cairn

Walk 3

Carnassarie
Castle

P

Kilmartin
Eye

Sheep fank

Cup-marked
Rock

Glenmoine

Walled
Garden

Upper Largie
Farm

Kilmartin
House
(demolished)

A816

Quarry

Garage

Glebe
Cairn

Kilmartin

Museum

Hotel

P

Church

Walk 1

0   0.5
Kilometres

Sheep at Carnassarie Castle

From Carnassarie car park, go through a stone 'squeeze stile' gate in the top right corner of the car park to a vehicle track; note the black-banded waymarker post used along this walk. The track gains some height and imposing Carnassarie Castle comes into view. Continue uphill; just 25 metres short of the entrance to the Castle grounds is a track junction where the Castle is signed straight on.

(Ormaig, walk 3, is to the left here signed Kilmartin).

Follow the steps and a stone-paved path leads up to the Castle entrance where you're immediately struck by its commanding location, overlooking Kilmartin Glen.

Carnassarie Castle

Carnassarie Castle History

The Castle was built between 1565 and 1572, with some late 17th century remodelling. But the building you see today is probably not the first dwelling or fortification on the site. A charter of 1436 records the granting of land and by 1529 it was included in land that passed to the Earls of Argyll as part of a marriage settlement. In 1559 the Earl granted land to Master John Carswell who was at the time rector of Kilmartin. The land grant included a Castle, which the present building replaced. Little remains of this earlier building, but there are traces of earlier structures on the site, including a possible Dun, which can be seen on a rocky outcrop to the north of the Castle.

John Carswell was evidently an ambitious man. By 1567 he became Bishop of the Isles. He had substantial resources and was very well connected, so was able to build this very impressive Castle, consisting of a tower and hall range. It is well preserved, with many architectural features remaining intact.

Bishop Carswell was also a Gaelic speaker and his linguistic skills were put to good use, for he translated the Book of

Common Order into Gaelic, which became the earliest printed book in Scots Gaelic.

Carswell died in 1572 and the Castle was held by his sons and grandsons until it passed into the Campbell family. During the 1644-46 civil conflicts it was garrisoned, unsurprising perhaps given its strategic location.

During the 9th Earl of Argyll's rebellion against the crown in 1685, the Castle was besieged and partly burned. From this time on it fell into disrepair, until being acquired from the Campbell family by Neil Malcolm of Poltalloch in 1829. By 1844 it was described as being in ruins, but it remained in the Malcolm family for a further hundred years or so until it was gifted to the nation. It is now in the care of Historic Scotland. There are information boards around the site to tell you more about the Castle's history and its architectural features.

The entrance to the Castle itself is to the right, in the north eastern corner, under an armorial panel which bears the motifs of the 5th Earl of Argyll (a galley) with those of Scotland (a lion rampant) representing his wife Jean Stewart. She was the natural daughter of James V of Scotland and half-sister of Mary Queen of Scots. There is also a Gaelic inscription, DIA LE UA NDUIBH(N)E 'God be with Ó Duibhne' (the head of the Campbell family).

Beneath the main stair at the entrance is a room with gun loops (small holes through which guns could be fired).

Steps lead up to the hall, which now overlooks the

Inside Carnassarie Castle

kitchen. In the hall you will be able to see many architectural fragments, family crests and armorial panels. The kitchen would have been stone vaulted. Look out for the oven within the huge fireplace. To the right of the fireplace is a water inlet and a sluice in a windowsill by the hearth which would have let dirty water outside. The rest of the ground floor would have been store rooms. In the cellar there is a now dry cistern.

There is a narrow stair, leading to the private family quarters. This had a garderobe (toilet) with a chute in the wall. Others can be seen in the walls too. You can see where the floors would have been from the position of the fireplaces in the walls. Climb the narrow spiral stairs to the wall heads. On the way, at the top of the first flight, you cross the private family quarters from where more steps lead to the top, with a great view down Kilmartin Glen and to the North.

Exterior of Carnassarie Castle

In the grounds of Carnassarie Castle

Retrace your steps to explore the garden, which has the remains of outbuildings, possibly stables. Look out for the cup marked rock, which dates from thousands of years earlier than the Castle, and which might have been brought here from elsewhere in the surrounding landscape.

A gate-arch on the west bears the initials S.D.C.-L.H.L., for Sir Duncan Campbell (of Achenbreck) and Lady Henrietta Lindsay his wife, and the date 1681. Sir Duncan was Keeper of the Castle in the 17th century and he was a supporter of the Earl of Argyll's rebellion.

Retrace your route to the car park.

To the north, you can see a massive Bronze Age burial cairn on the hill behind the Castle. This is called Cairnbaan (Gaelic for white cairn). You might spot two standing stones and a cairn, and there are other prehistoric monuments including rock art nearby.

Looking towards the cairn at Carnassarie

Optional Extension to Kilmartin

2.1 miles/3.4km one way to Kilmartin, 45 minutes to 1 hour walk. This extension is suitable for cycles as part of Sustrans route 78.

©David Lyons/kM

The setting of Carnassarie Castle

Turn right after descending the steps from the Castle and after 25 metres on your right is a signpost to Kilmartin. Follow the track which leads to a gate and continue on the track as it dog-legs around the edge of the field to a junction where you turn left for Kilmartin. With the village in view, the track descends between fields to a gate at the entrance to Largie Wood. Continue down, then pass through another gate. The track leads down the partly wooded glen; go through a gateway and right through another. Gain some height, past a large stone-walled enclosure which was formerly a walled garden.

The original Kilmartin House stood on this site, and the walled garden was part of its policies. Very little now remains of this Georgian Mansion House. Built around 1748, it was demolished in the mid 1800s. Many of the larger trees you see are remnants of the designed landscape of the Poltalloch Estate, which would have taken in most of the Glen in the earlier part of the 19th century.

Then the track follows a sinuous course, through a succession of gateways and soon affords good views across the glen to Kilmartin. Down just past some derelict stone buildings turn left at a junction. Approaching a working quarry the track bears right. Beyond the quarry turn left for Kilmartin (or go straight on for Dunadd walk 9). Continue along the wide track to the A816 road and turn right; walk beside the road for about 20 metres, passing the path which provides access to Kilmartin Glebe Cairn in the nearby field. Ascend the roadside path which takes you to Kilmartin Museum.

Upper Largie Quarry Prehistoric Site

The terrace at the head of Kilmartin Glen, now a working gravel quarry, was investigated by archaeologists before the quarry was opened. Some monuments were already known to exist there, but the investigations and subsequent excavations revealed a complex of ritual and burial sites that have changed our understanding of the internationally important archaeology in Kilmartin Glen.

As well as other monuments, this is also the site of Scotland's largest timber circle, but all traces have now been quarried away.

The view down Kilmartin Glen from Carnassarie Castle

NOTE: This walk links directly with 1 (and 7 and 10 – and even 13 to Crinan, and even further over Castle Dounie then along the cycle trail to Carsaig and Tayvallich!) and many may prefer to do the full through walk, saving Ormaig for a separate trip.

Cairns, rock art, standing stones and a henge

Grid reference at start and finish: NR 834 968 (OS 1:50,000 sheet 55)
Distance: 1.2 miles/2 km
Parking at start and finish: Eastern side of A816 road 1.5 miles/2.4
 km south of Kilmartin
Loop/There and back: There and back
Duration: 45 minutes – 1 hour
Terrain: Grass, paths, field with boggy patches after rain
Gradient: Flat throughout. Easy
Pushchair/Wheelchair friendly: In dry conditions only
Refreshments: At the Kilmartin Museum Café 01546 510278 or the
 Kilmartin Hotel 01546 510250
Toilets: Nearest public toilets next to the Kilmartin Hotel
Cycle path: No
Dog friendly: No

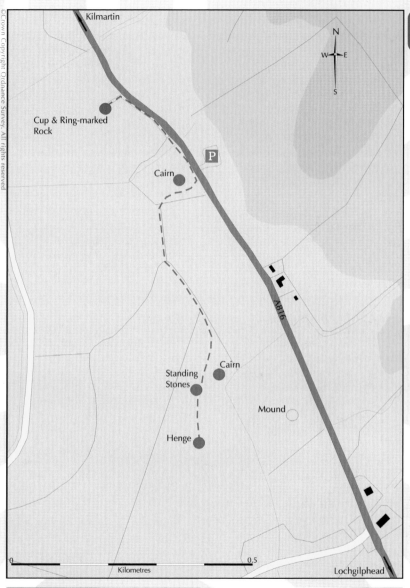

Kilmartin

Cup & Ring-marked
Rock

P

Cairn

A816

Standing
Stones

Cairn

Mound

Henge

0

0.5

Kilometres

Lochgilphead

From this walk you can take in an amazing variety of prehistoric monuments in a very small area. Their survival might in part be because they were a focus for the 'designed landscape' created by the Poltalloch Estate in the 19th century. But it is clear that the sites that remain are only a fraction of what was once here when Kilmartin was in its prehistoric 'heyday'.

From the car park cross the road with care and go through a small gate in the stone wall. A short path leads to Dunchraigaig cairn in front of you.

Dunchraigaig Cairn

This prehistoric burial cairn lies on a ridge (most likely a gravel terrace and/or raised beach) so it is elevated and looks out over the surrounding landscape. It has been excavated twice, in the 1860s and in the 1920s.

Although these excavators did not have access to the kind of techniques that archaeologists use today, both phases of work revealed that the site had been used for burials over a number of years.

The first burial was probably quite simple, dug into the natural ground surface, and a person laid inside. Later, a stone lined burial chamber, known as a cist, was built over this burial. Cremated human bone, flint chippings, and a decorated Food Vessel were found in this cist. A further burial was made at Dunchraigaig as a person was laid onto the upper cist slab. This is an unusual practice for the time. The slab is partially visible near the centre of the cairn.

The cairn also contained a second cist, which is now under the cairn material so

Dunchraigaig Cairn

cannot be seen. Cremated human remains and another decorated pot had been placed within it.

A third cist is still visible on the south east side of the cairn. The top slab is visible, but you can look into the cist as one of its side slabs is missing. The burnt and unburnt bones of at least 8 people had been laid into this cist. The deposits of bone had been carefully placed in discrete groups separated by small stones.

Other finds included pottery fragments, and a stone axe head, but sadly the whereabouts of this is now not known.

When Dunchraigaig Cairn was built, the rock art site had already been created. Such a massive cairn would have been erected for people of importance, and may have been sited near to older monuments, perhaps to draw on their power.

Food Vessel from Dunchraigaig Cairn

To reach the cup and ring marked rock outcrops from the eastern side of the cairn you walk northwards (towards Kilmartin) along a faint path between the trees. Step across a small burn and go up to a gate from where a fenced path, parallel to the road, leads on for nearly 300 metres, then turns sharp left down to the rock within a fenced enclosure; a small stile enables you to inspect it close up.

Baluachraig rock art

Baluachraig Rock Art

Three sections of bedrock are marked with very impressive rock art. The most common motif is the cup and ring mark, and this site is one of the more complex.

There are at least 140 cup marks on these stones, look out for the row of 10 cups, some of which have rings.

Some tentative evidence is beginning to emerge from recent work both here and further afield that earthfast rock art might belong to the late Neolithic period, making it one of the first monuments to be created in this particular group.

Retrace your steps to the cairn.

To visit Ballymeanoch standing stones, cairn and henge, walk west past Dunchraigaig cairn on your right, then go through a wooden gate on your left. Follow a fenced path between fields, traversing the edge of a bank overlooking a wide expanse of marshy ground. After about 100 metres the path bends through a gap in the stone wall. Continue to another gate into a large field.

Ballymeanoch Standing Stones (also known as Stone Rows)

This monument consists of two groups of stones standing in parallel lines. You will see six stones, but in prehistory there would have been at least one more – an outlier which fell some time in the late 19th century. Look out for the two cup and ring marked stones. It has been suggested that these stones might have once been earthfast rock art slabs which were then quarried to become standing stones; however not all agree with this theory. The seventh stone broke into pieces and the fragments lie nearby. This stone too is cup marked and it also had a large perforation through which, a local legend has it, people shook hands to seal a bargain. After the stone fell, the socket where it had once stood was excavated and patches of cremated human bone were found. This might constitute a deposit made just before the stone was erected. The bone has been carbon dated to between 1400 BC and 1050 BC, which is the Middle Bronze Age period.

The stones would have been part of a much larger ritual complex, as has been evidenced by recent archaeological survey work.

The stone rows are, today, a very impressive and imposing sight, and although we cannot know for sure, it is suggested that they were used for rituals and ceremonies. One suggestion has been put forward that these rows marked the position of the moon's rising and setting. One stone however is slightly offset from this alignment, but this could be explained as a miscalculation made when the row was erected. There is also some suggestion that they might have been located at one end of a processional avenue.

Ballymeanoch sunset

Cairn

Visible now only as a small ring of upright stones is the remains of a cairn. It would once have been a circular mound of stones, with a kerb of larger stones around the edges. The stones were probably removed for road or wall building in the past and the once circular monument has been cut through by a more modern drainage ditch. The site has not been excavated, but it probably dates to the Early Bronze Age, so it is possibly earlier than the standing stones, but later than the rock art.

The large turf covered mound and the stone and earth mounds you can see from the stone rows and the main road might be other burial monuments. Excavations at one site in the 1920s were not able to determine if this interpretation was correct or not.

Ballymeanoch standing stones and the remains of a cairn

To locate the henge: walk westwards along the southern fence of the field, about 25 metres in from the fence for about 120 metres. You should be able to spot the slightly raised bank of the henge as you approach it.

©David Lyons/KM

Ballymeanoch from the air

Henge

You might be familiar with the term henge because of that greatest of all prehistoric monuments, Stonehenge, a massive stone circle in Wiltshire. The term describes a particular kind of prehistoric monument that consists of an enclosure (built of banks of earth and ditches, or of stone) with entrances. So although the henge at Ballymeanoch and Stonehenge are very different in appearance, they both conform to this archaeological classification.

Ballymeanoch Henge consists of a circular earth embankment and ditch, about 42 metres diameter overall. There are entrances to the east and west. This is the only henge known in this part of Scotland. Most other henges date to the earlier Neolithic period, and were used for rituals, celebrations or ceremonies, but it has been suggested that the particular features of this site indicate that it might be Early Bronze Age. Evidence also demonstrates that it was a focus for burial for there are two stone lined cists dug into the centre. Upon excavation, one was found to have been disturbed, but the other contained a pottery vessel. The vessel was empty as it would have contained bones which decomposed long ago. The pot is of a style known as a Beaker and dates to between 2300 and 2000 BC. The pot is part of the collections of the British Museum, and on loan to Kilmartin Museum where you can see it on display. Both cists are still visible.

Although the henge is not as old as the rock art, it would have been still visible by the time the standing stones were erected.

Retrace your steps to the start.

Morning mist at Ballymeanoch

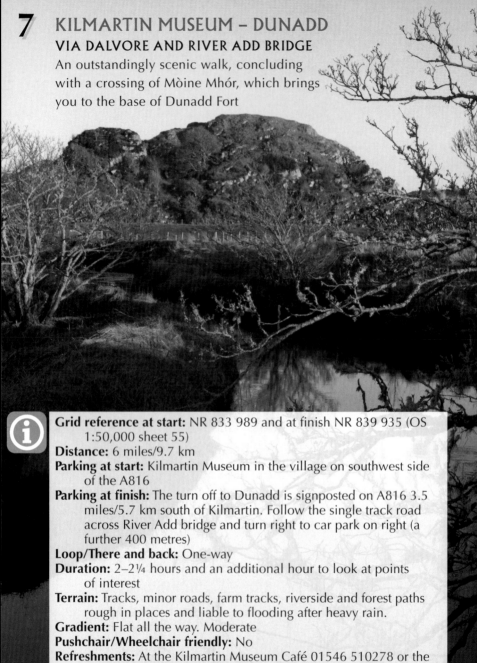

7 KILMARTIN MUSEUM – DUNADD
VIA DALVORE AND RIVER ADD BRIDGE

An outstandingly scenic walk, concluding
with a crossing of Mòine Mhór, which brings
you to the base of Dunadd Fort

Grid reference at start: NR 833 989 and at finish NR 839 935 (OS
1:50,000 sheet 55)

Distance: 6 miles/9.7 km

Parking at start: Kilmartin Museum in the village on southwest side
of the A816

Parking at finish: The turn off to Dunadd is signposted on A816 3.5
miles/5.7 km south of Kilmartin. Follow the single track road
across River Add bridge and turn right to car park on right (a
further 400 metres)

Loop/There and back: One-way

Duration: 2–2¼ hours and an additional hour to look at points
of interest

Terrain: Tracks, minor roads, farm tracks, riverside and forest paths
rough in places and liable to flooding after heavy rain.

Gradient: Flat all the way. Moderate

Pushchair/Wheelchair friendly: No

Refreshments: At the Kilmartin Museum Café 01546 510278 or the
Kilmartin Hotel 01546 510250

Toilets: Nearest public toilets next to the Kilmartin Hotel

Cycle path: No

Dog friendly: Under close control only

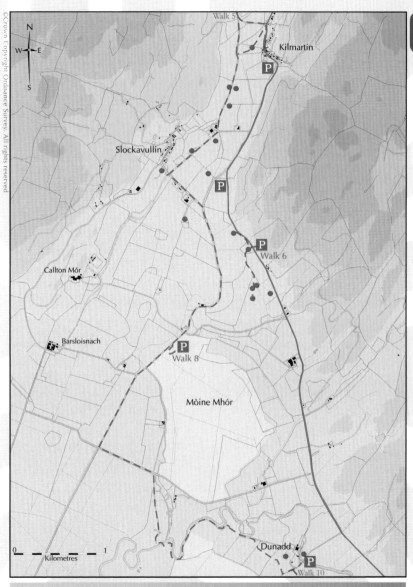

Walk 5

Kilmartin

P

Slockavullin

P

Walk 6

P

Callton Mór

Barsloisnach

P
Walk 8

Mòine Mhór

0   1
Kilometres

Dunadd
P
Walk 10

Moon over Dunadd

Follow the directions in walk 1 from Kilmartin to the T-junction 400 metres beyond Temple Wood, where Ri Cruin is to the left. Turn left and pass the access track to Ri Cruin. Continue along the road to the T-junction. Turn right and walk along the road for 3 km.

You will pass the Mòine Mhór (walk 8) on the way.

Kilmartin Glen is part of the Poltalloch Estate, which has influenced the landscape in a great many ways. On the road you will pass Luibs; these are cottages built to house estate workers. Further down the road you will pass East Lodge (built in 1854), the former eastern gatehouse to the now ruined Poltalloch House (sometimes known as Callton Mór). Across the road, opposite the lodge, you will see dips in the now tree covered ground and these are the remnants of the former Tileworks. Here clay was extracted for the making of drainage tiles and bricks for use on the Poltalloch Estate. On the hill to the right you will see the chapel of St Columba, built in 1854 as the chapel of the Malcolms of Poltalloch. The medieval Kilmichael Cross stood here before being moved to Kilmartin Museum.

©David Lyons/KM

Dunadd and the River Add from the air

©David Lyons/KM

Dunadd and the River Add

Further down the road there is a signpost to Barsloisnach (the home farm of the Poltalloch Estate). This lies near the impressive remains of the now ruined Poltalloch House built 1849-53. Please note that it is not possible to visit Poltalloch House – it is in an unstable and dangerous state. Continue down the road until you reach a junction signposted Drimvore, turn left here towards Dunadd and walk along this road for 600 metres.

Just short of a bridge over a tributary of the River Add, turn right along a farm track, signed Dunadd, which then comes into view on the left. The track may fade as you walk south across part of the Mòine Mhór – just aim for a ruined stone cottage ahead and you should come to some large flat stepping stones.

Cross the River Add on a small footbridge nearby to the left, then go along the riverbank path to a sign to Dunadd beside a sharp bend in the river. Cross stepping stones to the right and go left through a small gate and continue along the river bank, where stepping stones have been placed across areas liable to flooding.

Cross a small footbridge near a wide river bend then go right through a gate to a firm narrow path through a small area of young deciduous trees. From the far side of this fenced area continue along the riverside path to a gate on the right. Cross the field to a small gate, then through another field, always following signs for Dunadd. Go through another gate in a stone wall to a narrow, rough waymarked path and follow some stepping stones around the lowermost slopes of Dunadd. Descend to a good path, which you follow to a junction. Cairnbaan and Achnabreck are signed to the right (see walk 14 and walk 12). Dunadd car park is just 100 metres straight on. The footpath to Dunadd fort (walk 9) is directly opposite the car park, a visit to the site being a natural extension of this walk.

8 MÒINE MHÓR NATIONAL NATURE RESERVE TILEWORKS TRAIL

A unique peat bog and salt marsh

Grid reference at start and finish: NR 825 959 (OS 1:50,000 sheet 55)

Distance: 0.4 miles/0.6 km

Parking at start and finish: Designated area on the eastern side of B8025 road between Kilmartin and Bellanoch, immediately south of the junction of Long Walk road.

Loop/There and back: Loop

Duration: 30 minutes

Terrain: Firm, level path; optional section of level, secure duckboards

Gradient: Flat all the way. Easy

Pushchair/Wheelchair friendly: Yes

Refreshments: At the Kilmartin Museum Café 01546 510278 or the Kilmartin Hotel 01546 510250

Toilets: Nearest public toilets next to the Kilmartin Hotel

Cycle path: Yes

Dog friendly: Yes

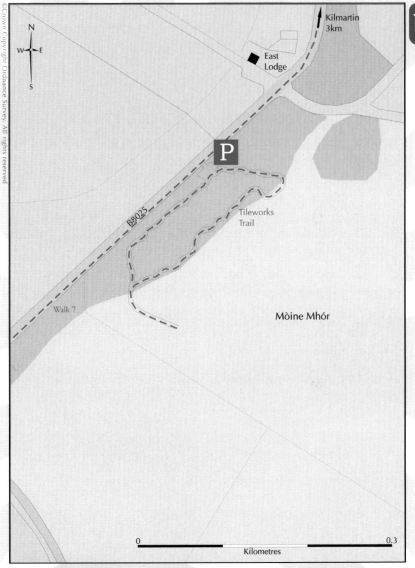

N
W—E
S

Kilmartin
3km

East
Lodge

P

B8025

Tileworks
Trail

Walk 7

Mòine Mhór

0   Kilometres   0.3

Information boards at the car park provide a helpful introduction to this walk which explores one of the last remaining raised peat bogs in Britain. There is a leaflet dispenser in the car park where you can pick up Scottish Natural Heritage leaflets with detailed information about the eight highlighted features of the Tileworks Trail.

From the car park set out along the woodland path to your left. Soon, as the path bends right the views open out across Mòine Mhór and you're warned about the hazards of walking across the bogland. There are many hidden holes and deep drains so please be careful!

The contrast between the almost luxuriant mosses, lichens, trees and ferns of the woodland and the seemingly monotonous bogland is particularly striking. However, as you'll soon learn, many species of plants as well as insects live on the Great Moss.

At a minor junction, just past point 5, bear left to a boardwalk which leads to a viewing platform right out on the Great Moss. The isolated hill straight ahead, beyond the Moss, is Dunadd (see walk 9).

Return to the main path and continue past two more information points to the car park.

There is an interesting art work here which was created by local school pupils as part of a project to help them better understand the rich natural heritage of the area.

Along the Tileworks Trail

The Mòine Mhór (Gaelic – big moss/bog), sometimes known as the Crinan Moss, is an amazingly diverse place, a wild landscape of hummocks, hollows and pools, teeming with life. The bog is formed from plant matter – as it dies lack of oxygen prevents it from fully decaying. Sphagnum moss soaks up water and holds it like a sponge, and other water loving plants are able to thrive. Peat forms at about 1mm a year and the Mòine Mhór is now raised in a peaty dome which in places is around 4 metres deep. The dome is clearly visible from many viewpoints in the glen. You can get a really good view of the Mòine Mhór from the top of Dunadd (walk 9).

The Mòine Mhór from Dunadd

Looking across the Mòine Mhór towards Dunadd

Towards the Crinan Estuary the bog gradually changes to salt marsh, creating a unique environment that is home to many rare species. These include hen harriers which can be seen quartering the Moss looking for a meal. Red squirrels can occasionally be seen in the native woodland on the road fringes of the Moss. In spring you might see a profusion of toads on the move after a long winter sleep, heading for their breeding pools. Newts can also be found here, but they are harder to spot, as is the elusive slow worm. During the late spring months the fluffy flowers of cotton grass carpet the bog like snow. Visiting whinchats join the resident stonechats and meadow pipits on the bog and the woodlands are full of willow warblers. In summer yellow star flowers of bog asphodel light up the bogland while dragonflies and the beautiful demoiselle dance

Heather in flower

Osprey over the River Add

in the air, their wings catching the sun. 10 different species can be spotted here. Towards the river and the estuary ospreys are a common sight. As the year wears on and autumn comes, the Moss changes its colours to burnt oranges, reds and purples, which are complemented by the autumn foliage of the oak and alder woodland. Look out for shy roe and the non-native sika deer around the fringes of the reserve. Winter is a busy time for bird life as large numbers of wildfowl congregate on the estuary and surrounding fields. These include whooper swans, Greenland white-fronted geese and wigeon. The frost-sparkled sphagnum is beautiful in the bogland in winter and the reserve is an ideal place for quiet contemplative walks.

But the place has not always been quiet and peaceful. In the 19th century the Poltalloch Estate began an impressive and ambitious programme of land improvements. Roads were built over the Moss and bridges over the River Add. Ditches were dug into the Moss, draining water to create productive agricultural land. The Tileworks

Sika deer

gets its name from this time as the deposits of clay found here were used to make field drains. Bricks were also made here, and there are a handful of brick built houses dating from the early 1850s in the Glen. Peat was an important source of fuel for folk living in this area for hundreds of years, and you can see old peat banks near the turn for Barsloisnach. In some places, as the peat was stripped, the prehistoric landscape it had hidden was once again revealed, for, as ancient as it seems, the bog hasn't always been here. Although we are not sure exactly when the Moss began to form, it is thought that a small bog was present around the time that people first began to farm and build monuments in the area, between 5,000 and 4,000 years ago. About 3,000 years ago there is evidence that the climate deteriorated and became wetter, which is thought to have triggered an expansion of peat bogs in many parts of western Britain. People had been living, farming and burying their dead in Kilmartin Glen for perhaps 2,000 years by then and in places standing stones they erected can still be seen poking out of the peat.

Golden-ringed dragonfly

9 DUNADD
Seat of the Kings of Dál Riata

Grid reference at start and finish: NR 839 935 (OS 1:50,000 sheet 55)

Distance: 0.2 miles/0.3 km

Parking at start and finish: Dunadd is signposted on the A816 3.5 miles/5.7 km south of Kilmartin; turn off the main A816 and follow the single track road across the River Add bridge, then turn right to the car park on the right (a further 400 metres)

Loop/There and back: There and back

Duration: 30 – 40 minutes

Terrain: Mostly rocky paths with short stretches across grass

Gradient: Steep ascent almost all the way to the summit, 55m above sea level. Moderate to hard (but short!)

Pushchair/Wheelchair friendly: No

Refreshments: At the Kilmartin Museum Café 01546 510278, the Kilmartin Hotel 01546 510250 or the Horseshoe Inn[1] in Bridgend 01546 606369

Toilets: Nearest public toilets next to the Kilmartin Hotel

Cycle path: No

Dog friendly: On lead only

[1]Interestingly, you can see the top half of two rotary quern stones built into the hearth of the bar of the Horseshoe Inn. One is certainly Early Medieval in date, and may even have come from Dunadd!

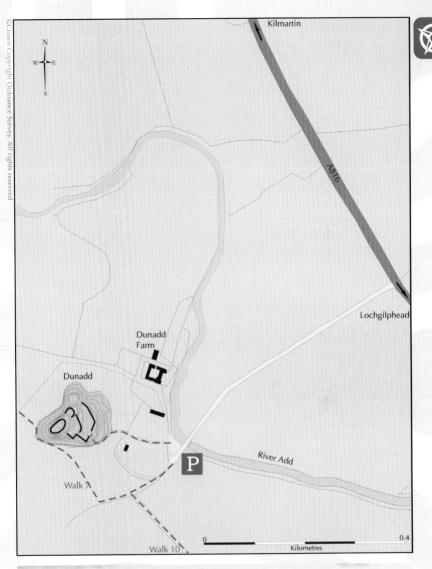

Kilmartin

A816

Lochgilphead

Dunadd
Farm

Dunadd

River Add

P

Walk 7

Walk 10

0   Kilometres   0.4

Dunadd seen from the east

The rocky hill rising out of the flat plain of the River Add Basin might seem remote and uninhabited today, but the story of Dunadd is integral to the making of the nation, and so it is one of the most important archaeological sites in Scotland.

Some of the earliest documentary sources in Scottish and Irish literature shed light on Argyll and Dunadd, and its fascinating story has been revealed through several excavations.

This rocky crag was first fortified about 2,400 years ago. Already a site of some prominence, about 600 AD it became the most important place in the region for it was chosen as the seat of the Kings of Dál Riata – one of the most powerful kingdoms of its time.

Traditionally it was thought that the Kingdom was founded by Gaelic speaking Irish. But archaeologists now believe that Gaelic was the native language of the region, and that there was no invasion from Ireland.

Dunadd became a major political centre, making diplomatic contacts, and sometimes political alliances, with all the other major kingdoms of the day. But this was also a warrior culture. At times the Kings of Dál Riata engaged in warfare with their neighbours, and amongst themselves.

Dunadd was a centre of trade and imported many goods such as dyes from France, and exotic spices and wines. Shallow drafted ships negotiated their way up the River Add, connecting the Kings of Dál Riata to the rest of Europe. Christianity was beginning to spread at that time, and the Kings were certainly in contact with Iona, one of the most important Christian centres in western Europe.

The lower slopes of Dunadd

The inauguration stone at Dunadd

This was a stronghold from which to launch campaigns but it was also a symbolic and ritual centre where Kings – chosen from a group of eligible nobles – were literally made. Carvings on the rocks near the summit of Dunadd are thought to have been used in pagan inauguration ceremonies that conferred kingly status upon an individual. The Church cleverly manoeuvred themselves into a central role in these rituals – thus conferring great political power upon themselves.

By the end of the 9th century, Dál Riata and the Pictish kingdom were united into the new kingdom of Alba (Scotland). The capital shifted to the east, and Dunadd, although not completely abandoned, ceased to be the power base of the region.

Before you set out, check the information boards in the car park.

Cross the farm access track then follow the grass and gravel path uphill for about 75 metres to a gate. The path becomes steeper and rougher as it twists and turns up through the boulder-strewn flanks of the hill.

There's a brief respite as you cross a relatively flat grassy area which is worth exploring.

Walk through the entrance way on your right to the first fortified level of the fort. This entrance, created from a natural fissure in the rock, has been designed deliberately to impress. In this way, the builders of Dunadd used the landscape to symbolically express the power and status of their King.

The excavations found traces of wooden buildings in this enclosure – possibly the remains of workshops where gold, silver, bronze and iron were worked.

The production of precious jewellery would have been under the control of the King at that time and gifts of metal objects were used to seal alliances and create obligations to provide fighting men and ships.

Explore the fortifications and look out for the well (now dry) which would have supplied the entire fort, people and animals, with fresh water. This can be found to the north of this enclosure.

A further scramble from the south side of the terrace leads to a rock sheet where you will find the carvings of a boar, two foot prints, a piece of Ogham script and, nearby, a rock cut basin. The rock surface has now been given a protective coating to prevent weathering, so you are looking at a replica of the carving, the real surface is hidden underneath. Along with documentary evidence, this combination of carvings points to Dunadd having been used as the place of inauguration of the Kings of Dál Riata. The use of footprints in inauguration ceremonies in the early medieval period is documented. The rock cut basin might be a very large prehistoric cup mark, or may have been recut from an earlier cup mark.

| a | Carvings |
| b | Well |

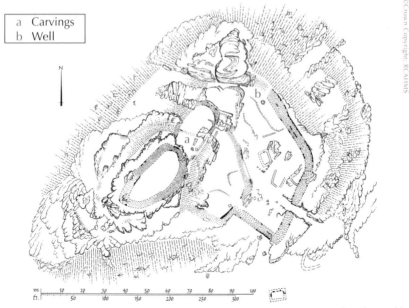

©Crown Copyright: RCAHMS

A plan of Dunadd

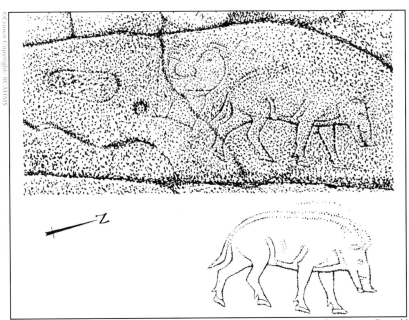

Carvings on Dunadd

The significance of the boar carving has been much debated. It is generally accepted to date to somewhere around the 7th and 8th centuries. Some have suggested the style of carving is Pictish, and that it was carved following the recorded Pictish conquest of Dunadd in 736, but then recut to resemble a domestic pig when the fortress was retaken. But if it was a symbol of Pictish conquest, the Kings of Dál Riata might simply have ordered it to be obliterated from their inauguration site, rather than alter it. So, it seems more likely to have been a carving made by the inhabitants of Dunadd themselves. Possibly the boar held totemic status within the Kingdom of Dál Riata?

The meaning of the Ogham script has been much debated too. Ogham is a form of writing used by both the Picts and people living in Dál Riata. The upper line is badly damaged and difficult to read. The lower line can be read with greater confidence (as 'VUORRMONAI') but the inscription remains difficult to interpret. The Ogham alphabet was used in Scotland from the 5th century until the 10th or 11th, and a date in the middle of this range is perhaps most likely for the Dunadd inscription.

It's only a short haul from there to the flattish, grassed summit.

From here you will have a fantastic view of the surrounding landscape. On a clear day you might be able to see the top of Ben Cruachan and the Paps of Jura. Looking to the south east, you will see the River Add as it makes its sinuous journey from Kilmichael Glen around Dunadd out to Crinan, with Jura in the distance. Traces of old river meanders are clear in the fields to the north. To the south, you will see a now fallen standing stone in the field next to the river and in the distance to the south you might be able to see others. The standing stone in the garden of Dunadd Farm house next to a tree was recently erected! You will also be able to see an exceptionally panoramic view of the Mòine Mhór (walk 8) and buildings along the Crinan Canal (walk 13).

The natural features of mountains, the rocky summit itself, and the close proximity to prehistoric monuments combined to make Dunadd the perfect site for the regional capital. But Dunadd was not the only fortification in the area, for in the hills around there are other forts and duns. You can also see Duntrune, a later medieval castle guarding the Crinan Estuary from the summit.

Around the edges of the summit you will see some of the remains of the summit fort – a building which had several phases of construction. The western face is very steep, best viewed from above.

©David Lyons/kM

Aerial view of Dunadd

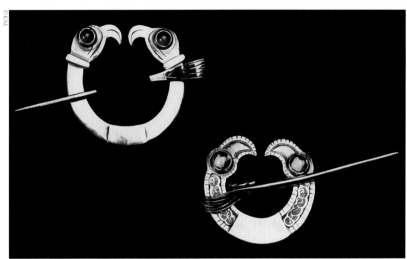

Modern replicas of brooches found at Dunadd

Early morning on Dunadd

Retrace your steps to the car park, taking care on the descent as some of the rocks can be very slippery.

Grid reference at start and finish: NR 839 935, and NR 823 910 (OS 1:50,000, sheet 55)

Distance: 2.5 miles/4 km

Parking at start: At Dunadd, signposted on A816 3.5 miles/5.7 km south of Kilmartin; turn off A816 and follow single track road, across River Add bridge, then right to the car park on the right (a further 400 metres).

Parking at finish: Forestry Commission Dunardry car park on south side of B841, 1 mile/1.5 km west of Cairnbaan

Loop/There and back: One-way

Duration: 1½ – 1¾ hours

Terrain: Potentially muddy farm tracks, paths with stepping stones and boardwalks in places, generally rough, muddy in places, some liable to flooding after heavy rain.

Gradient: A few short ups and downs, some steep. Moderate

Pushchair/Wheelchair friendly: No

Refreshments: At the Cairnbaan Hotel 01546 603668

Toilets: Nearest public toilets at Front Green, Lochgilphead

Cycle path: No

Dog friendly: Under close control only

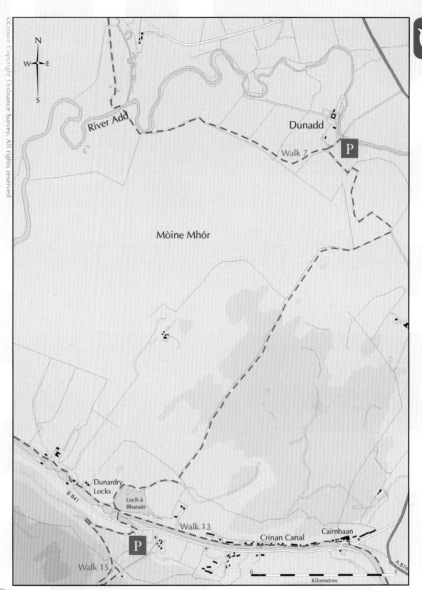

This path was created as a walking route by the Dalriada Project, a recent Heritage Lottery Funded landscape partnership scheme. It links two of the area's most important monuments, Dunadd (walk 9) and the Crinan Canal (walk 13). This is a route that takes you through beautiful oak woods as well as more recent non-native forestry plantation.

10 DUNADD CAR PARK TO DUNARDRY

Although this walk is described as one-way only, it may of course be more convenient to walk there and back, making an easy day walk or a brisk half-day outing.

From Dunadd car park, turn right from the access road, as signposted for Cairnbaan. Here a signpost tells you about the Dalriada Heritage Trail, of which this is part. Just 100 metres along, turn left through a gate along a farm track towards Cairnbaan. Beyond another gate after 200 metres the track bends right and rises slightly to a left turn from where it may be very muddy, depending on the weather and the activities of any cattle in the field. The track crosses the slope and descends to a gate. Almost immediately turn right towards Cairnbaan, crossing a burn on stepping stones, which may be under water after prolonged heavy rain.

Continue past fairly recently planted deciduous trees then conifers on the left with moorland beyond on the right. The views north to Dunadd across Mòine Mhór are excellent. Conifers on the left give way to deciduous species, mainly birch. After about 200 metres beside a stone wall on the right, the path starts to bend to the left through woodland, predominantly oaks. The path can be wet and boggy here and there; you'll encounter the first of many sections of boardwalk, most firm and reliable, though some (comprising two parallel planks) need to be taken carefully if they're wet. The clearly defined path makes its way generally south west for about 1.5 miles/2.4 km through woodland, past a small area of conifers and across moorland dotted with birches.

Woodland near Dunadd

On the trail near Dunardry

A distinct downhill stretch leads to open ground where you'll find a sign to Cairnbaan; turn right along an old forest track for about 200 metres, then bear right along a waymarked path, just past another Cairnbaan sign. This short muddy path leads to a flight of stone steps, more muddy path then a dry descent through tall conifers to stepping stones beside Loch a' Bharain, which was dammed to form an overflow for the Crinan Canal. Cross a weir gate, used to control water levels, then go up right to a path. Continue down to a gate and the Crinan Canal and the nearby path. Signposts indicate the direction towards the Dunardry car park. Cross over the lock gate of canal Lock 9 to join the B841 road. Turn left and walk along the road for about 100 metres, from where you will see the access road to the car park.

11 KILMICHAEL GLEN

Medieval gravestones, various rock art sites, standing stones and a crannog

Grid reference at start and finish: NR 859 935 (OS 1:50,000 sheet 55)

Distance: 7 miles/11.4 km – this walk also forms part of a circular cycle route that takes in Kilmichael Glen, Carnassarie Castle, Kilmartin Glen, the Mòine Mhór, and the Crinan Canal. The distance for the cycle route is 20 miles/32 km. See below for more details.

Parking at start and finish: Turn off the A816 road 1.5 miles/2.5 km north of the B841 junction or 4.3 miles (7 km) south of Kilmartin along a minor road signposted for Kilmichael Glen. Take the third left turn towards 'Kilmichael Glen' and continue to the village of Kilmichael Glassary (0.6 miles/1km from the A816). The car park is on the left at a minor junction, beside the school and opposite the prominent Church. Please respect the school's need for this car park and use it only outwith school hours.

Loop/There and back: There and back

Duration: 3 – 3½ hours

Terrain: Short informal, grassy path from minor road to rock art site, otherwise all on minor roads

Gradient: More or less level. Easy - moderate

Pushchair/Wheelchair friendly: Yes, except access to rock art site

Refreshments: At the Horseshoe Inn in Bridgend 01546 606369

Toilets: Nearest public toilets at Front Green, Lochgilphead

Cycle path: Suitable for cycles, except for access to rock art site.

Dog friendly: Yes, on leads throughout

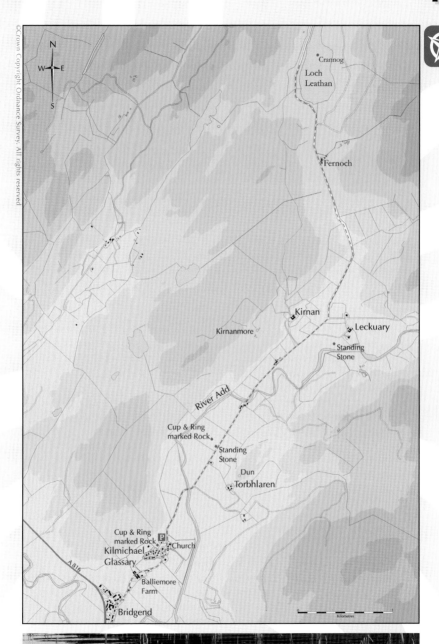

N
W E
S

Crannog
Loch
Leathan

Fernoch

Kirnan

Leckuary

Kirnanmore

Standing
Stone

River Add

Cup & Ring
marked Rock

Standing
Stone

Dun
Torbhlaren

Cup & Ring
marked Rock
Kilmichael
Glassary

Church

A 816

Balliemore
Farm

Bridgend

Kilometres

Like Kilmartin Glen, Kilmichael Glen has a wealth of prehistoric sites. You can explore many of them along the route. The River Add flows down Kilmichael Glen, to meander around Dunadd, just after which it is joined by the Kilmartin Burn, and empties into the sea at Loch Crinan.

The name 'Bridgend' is marked on the first edition Ordnance Survey map, based on a survey of 1865. The main road now diverts away from the old bridge, built in 1737, from which the village takes its name.

The fields around here were the site of the 'Kilmichael Tryst', or 'The Black Fair', an annual cattle and hiring fair. Cattle were driven from here, from the surrounding area, and from Jura, Colonsay and Islay, having first been ferried across to North Knapdale. They were then gathered and driven on to the markets in the south east of Scotland, a practice that effectively ended in the 1880s when the railway came to Oban. The Horseshoe Inn dates to the early 19th century.

To begin the walk you can park in Bridgend and walk up the road from here, or drive along the road signposted Kilmichael Glen.

If you choose to walk from Bridgend, you will pass through a farm which is called Balliemore. This is a typical example of a mid 19th century 'improved' farm. Built by the Poltalloch Estate, the house and farm buildings would have included amenities such as a dairy, a washhouse and peat store. The farm is private.

Continuing up the road, you will pass the gates of the former manse, built 1838 – 40 (now a private house), beyond which is an even older cottage. Next to that is the walled garden of the former manse, now the site of the present day manse. Next to this is the Steading (recently converted to a private house) which contained the manse's stables, byre, dairy and piggery. Just before the Church there is a formerly three storied structure that housed farm workers and the former village lock-up (also recently converted to a private house).

On the opposite side of the road there is the former schoolhouse and Glassary Primary School (built in 1876). Adjoining this is the school car park.

The first of several sites to visit is the cup and ring marked rocks. These are clearly signposted from the car park as 'Kilmichael Glassary Inscribed Rocks'. Here you'll find an information board. Walk up the side road for about 40 metres to the far end of the field on the right. Go through the kissing gate and follow the informal path to the enclosure protecting the rock art. Climb the stile over the upper side of the fence.

Kilmichael Glassary rock art

Kilmichael Glassary Rock Art

Within the fenced enclosure, you will see two groups of cup and ring markings carved onto earthfast rock slabs. There are many single cups, as well as cups with rings and gutters. Look out for the cups with rings shaped like a keyhole, which occur on both slabs. Some of the outcrops around the fenced enclosure also have markings, but please don't be tempted to pull back the vegetation as the carvings are liable to be damaged by stock.

Return to the main road and cross over to the entrance to Glassary Parish Church.

Glassary Parish Church

The 'Kil' element in the place name Kilmichael Glassary indicates there was an early Christian settlement in the Glen. Glassary was the chapel-at-ease for Kilneuair, on Loch Awe, until the extensive parish was divided in the 17th century. The existing building dates to 1873, and is at least the third Church to have stood on this spot.

In the graveyard you'll find medieval carved grave slabs. These are on the left, a few steps from the path just before the ramp to the Church entrance. There are over 20 14th to 15th century stones in this graveyard. Between the eastern wall of the Church and the stone wall enclosing the graveyard you will find parts of 15th century box tombs which have been reused. One tomb chest slab refers to a local resident 'Here lies Alexander MacIver of Kirnan' – MacIver held lands here in the 16th century. People who claim Alexander as a relative still live in Kilmichael Glen. You will also see the tomb of Duncan Roy, son of Alan MacLachlan, or 'Ruaraidh Mac', as he is known locally.

Look out for the early Christian stone to the right of the gate, which bears a Latin ring headed cross.

Many of the stones at Glassary are now buried in the grass. Dunadd Historic Gravestones Group is working on finding ways to best preserve them. You are liable to cause the stones permanent damage if you attempt to remove the grass so please do not be tempted.

Glassary Parish Church

Follow the road northeast out of the village up Kilmichael Glen.

Cross the bridge, built in the 19th century, and continue past a track on the right marked Torbhlaren. It was on this farm in 1814 that a richly decorated 12th century bell shrine was found. The remains of an iron bell thought to date to the 7th century were discovered inside the shrine. On the high hill against which Torbhlaren Farmhouse nestles is a Dun of the same name. Little of this site now remains visible, much of the walls having been robbed of stone.

About 1.1km from the car park, you'll draw level with a tall standing stone in the field on your left.

Torbhlaren standing stone

The standing stone bears cup marks, similar to the stone settings at Ballymeanoch and Nether Largie, and might similarly date to the Middle Bronze Age. One more stone is known to have stood in the field, and there might have been others. In the field you will see two earthfast rock outcrops, which are covered with cup and ring marks.

Recent excavations found hammer stones and charcoal which was carbon dated to between 2920 BC and 2760 BC, suggesting the rock art is late Neolithic. Paleoenvironmental work undertaken as part of the same project found evidence that people were farming this Glen in the very early Neolithic period.

The River Add would have once cut a more sinuous path down Kilmichael Glen. As with the Kilmartin Burn it has been straightened and deepened in places in an attempt to prevent flooding. Much more water would have flowed down this River before the hydroelectric scheme was built on Loch Glashan in the 1960s and now much of the water that empties from this loch is diverted into Loch Fyne.

Continue along the road – you will cross a bridge, proceed until you reach the gates for Kirnan. Built as a hunting lodge, Kirnan is

Rock art on the Torbhlaren outcrops

now a private residence. On the hill around the house you will see rhododendrons which are the remains of a formal garden created by botanist Robert Heber Macaulay in 1897. Two township settlements Kirnan More and Kirnan Beg, abandoned in the 1860s, are close by.

Further along the road you will see a farm gate marked Leckuary. In the fields is a standing stone known as AnCar, now leaning at an angle. Please call at the farm house if you wish to get closer to this stone.

Approximately 1.2 km further on the road bears left. As the Glen narrows you begin to climb uphill. There are stands of forestry and new planting on both sides. On the right hand side of the road you pass Fernoch, now private houses but initially built to house forestry workers.

You reach the south shore of Loch Leathan, about 2 km from the junction. The crannog is visible from here but it's worth continuing to a point opposite the islet to better see its features.

You will pass through areas of newly planted ground. Survey work undertaken by Kilmartin Museum prior to the planting revealed the remains of several settlements strung along the hill above you on the left, as well as several rock art sites, indicating different land uses in the past.

Loch Leathan Crannog

The crannog appears as a stony island above the water line of the Loch. This island is artificial, although its builders might have built upon a natural rock outcrop. The age of the site is not certain, however, a wooden circular hut might have stood on the site 2,000 years ago. There are traces of a stone built house. This might date to the 16th century, for a map of this date notes a building here.

In more recent times shooting hides were built, and these have obscured the ancient and historical features. Tradition has it that arrows were fired upon Alexander McDonald from here, during the civil wars in 1647, when he and his clan were spoiling Campbell lands.

Loch Leathen Crannog

Simply retrace your steps to the start, enjoying quite different views on the way.

Loop Cycle

This walk can also form the basis for a very enjoyable cycle ride suitable for mountain bikes, hybrids or tourers but not for road bikes. After studying the crannog continue to cycle up Kilmichael Glen. 300 metres from the end of the Loch there is a standing stone on your left but this is a fake! It was erected in 2010 to mark the creation of the track that goes up the hill. You will be passing through unfenced farmland and it is not advisable to take dogs during lambing or calving time.

Continue on this road past Barmolloch and Stroneskar until you reach a T junction. You will pass through three road gates – please make sure you close these gates. At the end of the Glen road, turn left onto the B840 (standing stones and a cairn on the left). Follow the B840 for approximately 1 mile and at the end turn left on to the A816. After approximately 800 metres you will pass the car park at Carnassarie Castle (walks 3 and 5).

You either cycle down the main A816 road, through Kilmartin to Bridgend, or use some of the other walks in this Guide to extend your cycle.

12 ACHNABRECK
(ALSO SPELT ACHNABREAC)
An unusually large group of prehistoric rock art outcrops

Grid reference at start and finish: NR 852 908 (OS 1:50,000 sheet 55)
Distance: 1.5 miles/2.4 km
Parking at start and finish: 200 yards/0.3km north of A816/B841
    junction (2.1 miles/3.3km north of Lochgilphead) turn off
    along a vehicle track signed Historic Scotland - 'Achnabreck'.
    Continue along the track, ignoring the road to the right to
    the kennels, for 500 metres until you reach the Forestry
    Commission car park on the right.
Loop/There and back: Loop
Duration: 45 minutes – 1 hour
Terrain: Paths and forest track
Gradient: Steady ascent and descent; approx height gain 80m. Easy-
    moderate
Pushchair/Wheelchair friendly: No
Refreshments: At the Cairnbaan Hotel 01546 603668
Toilets: Nearest public toilets at Front Green, Lochgilphead
Cycle path: No – although the walk crosses the Fire Tower Cycle
    Trail which has a number of options. For more information visit
    www.forestry.gov.uk.
Dog friendly: Yes

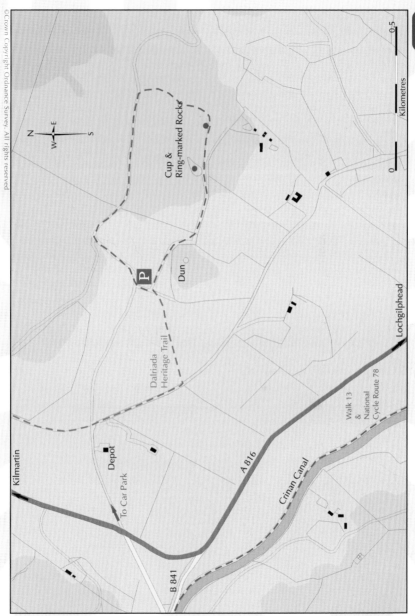

N
W—E
S

Cup &
Ring-marked Rocks

P

Dun

Dalriada
Heritage Trail

Kilmartin

Depot

To Car Park

B 841

A 816

Crinan Canal

Walk 13
&
National
Cycle Route 78

Lochgilphead

0   0.5
Kilometres

133

The group of carvings at this site is the largest of its kind in Europe. The name Achnabreac is Gaelic, and it might contain elements that mean 'speckled', which might be referring to the rock art? Three main outcrops are easily visited, but there are other carvings and prehistoric monuments in the area.

There are various information boards at the car park; the main one 'Achnabreac' has a map showing the colour-coded trails in the area. This walk follows the route of the yellow waymarked Achnabreac Trail.

Start on the eastern side of the car park where there are three information boards. Take the path to the north and begin to ascend gently. Pass junctions with tracks which lead off to the left and right.

About 500 metres from the start, and in the open, you reach a fence around a domed decorated rock surface. A warning sign asks you to keep outside the fence to protect the fragile rock art consisting of numerous cup and ring marks, individual cups and gutters running down the slope. The rock is epidiorite, a metamorphosed volcanic rock, which has been smoothed and polished by ice action. Broad grooves, running south east to north west along the slope of the surface, were produced by glacial erosion. Follow the board walk to the far end of the fence where there are good views to the south across Loch Gilp and Loch Fyne. It is possible to see as far as Arran on a clear day. It is worth walking round the outside of the fenced enclosure to see the rock surface from different directions.

The lower Western Outcrop at Achnabreck

Western Outcrop

From the site there are extensive views to Lochgilphead and Loch Fyne, west to the sea and Cairnbaan. The panoramic views might have been one reason why this place was chosen for such elaborate carvings. It is possible that trees were cleared to expose the view, for the landscape was at least partly wooded at that time. The rock surface itself has been scored by ice from the last glaciation, thousands of years before it was carved by humans.

The rock surface has eroded in places and some of the carvings are quite shallow, making them hard to see. So, the best time to visit is early in the morning, or in the evening, when the sun is low on the horizon. Rain water too can help make the carving more visible.

The most common motif on all the surfaces you can see is the cup and ring mark. Some motifs have had other elements added at a later date. In places it is even possible to detect individual 'peck' marks.

The first outcrop is enclosed by a metal fence to protect them. These carvings are thought to form three distinct groups. Look out for the line of four very large cup marks on the first sloping surface you see.

A warning sign asks you to keep outside the fence to protect the fragile rock art.

There are carvings on the top of the rock surface which you cannot see from outside the fence. At the centre of this group of carvings is the largest cup and ring marking in Scotland; formed of seven rings it measures nearly one metre in diameter. There is also a very rare motif known as the horned spiral, which appears again linked to another spiral on this surface. There are other rare motifs to the south of this group; a ringed enclosure, and a double groove on a cup and ring mark. Spirals are often seen on Irish burial chambers, and there is a spiral carved onto one of the stones at Temple Wood, suggesting a link.

It is possible that there is more rock art but we would ask that you do not hunt for it as this might cause damage.

From the end of the boardwalk, continue uphill for a few hundred metres to another smaller, also fenced, decorated rock surface, from where there's an even better view than at the previous site.

The upper rock surface at Achnabreck

The view from Achnabreck

The Eastern Outcrop at Achnabreck

Eastern outcrop

This rock surface is less extensively carved than the outcrop you have just left. Look out for the pear shaped cup and ring motif, and notice that all the ducts 'flow' in the same direction as the slope of the rock surface.

The path gains height to a picnic table with a fine outlook. Return the way you have come to the car park. Alternatively continue along this path, which bears to the left and meets the junction with the forest road. Turn left and continue along this road for 600 metres until you reach the car park on your left.

DUNARDRY BRIDGE

'Oh! The Crinan Canal for me
I don't like the wild raging sea
Them big foamin' breakers
Wad gie ye the shakers
The Crinan Canal for me'

Chorus from *The Song of the Puffermen* from the short stories of Neil
Munro, creator of the Vital Spark, a fictional Clyde Puffer, later immortalised

Introduction

Rightly described as Scotland's most beautiful shortcut, the Crinan Canal is a 9 mile (14.5) kilometre shortcut for seagoing vessels, avoiding the 100 mile passage through the dangerous waters round the Mull of Kintyre.

Starting in the Canal Basin at Ardrishaig, overlooking Loch Gilp, the route of the Canal passes through native woodlands to the narrow gap of hills at Cairnbaan, then along the foot of the Knapdale hills, and out into the open country of the Crinan Estuary. From here on spectacular views are to be had. Across the Mòine Mhór, you can see the hill of Dunadd, seat of the Kings of Dál Riata, around which the River Add flows and joins the sea at Crinan. The narrow gap here is guarded by Duntrune Castle on the opposite side of the loch. The real treat at the end of the Canal is the views out over the Sound of Jura. The Islands of Jura and Scarba can be seen in the distance and, on a clear day, Ben More on Mull can also be glimpsed to the north. There are many chances to spot Scotland's native wildlife along the route. Sea and estuary birds are the most commonly seen, especially wading birds, feeding on the rich mud of the tidal estuary. If you are really lucky, you might spot a hunting osprey. Along the grassy sides of the towpath, depending on the season, there is an abundance of wild flowers.

History of the Canal

Proposals had been made in the late 1700s for a shortcut for commercial sea going vessels between the Clyde and the west coast of Scotland that would avoid the risky waters around the Mull of Kintyre. A route was decided, civil engineer John Rennie appointed, and the considerable sum of £150,000 raised. Work began in September 1794. But all did not go according to the original plan. The terrain was difficult, and several attempts were made to complete the project. A disastrous flood in 1805 destroyed a large section of completed Canal, and the project was beset by financial concerns. Eventually, the Crinan Canal was declared open in 1809, some 10 years later than originally planned. Shortly after, the famous engineer Thomas Telford reported that repairs were needed. He undertook the work with customary briskness and the Canal reopened in 1817, 23 years after work first began.

The completed Canal has 15 locks including two sea locks, as well as numerous bridges and keepers' cottages along its length. It climbs to a height of just over 19 metres above sea level at the summit reach between Cairnbaan and Dunardry. Although repaired, most of the lock chambers and the Canal itself date to the late 18th century. Many of the original structures associated with the Canal, including bridges and locks, have been modified and improved over the last 150 years, with most dating to the first half of the 19th century.

The coming of the Canal would have had a profound impact on the area, in both social and economic terms. Over the years it took to fully complete, workers would have been brought into the area. Locals would also have found employment – gruelling labour perhaps, but welcome money for most families. The village of Ardrishaig developed because of the Canal, as did other businesses along the way, principally inns to accommodate travellers.

As a spin off from the Clyde paddle steamers taking holiday makers 'doon the watter', the Crinan Canal too had a paddle steamer. The Linnet took passengers along its length. As well as commercial sailing vessels, from the 1870s coal fired 'Clyde Puffers' used the route, providing a vital supply link to the West Coast and Hebridean Islands. Clyde Puffers were made famous by Inveraray born writer Neil Munro's tales of the escapades of the crew of the 'Vital Spark'.

In 1962, the Crinan Canal became the responsibility of the former British Waterways, now Scottish Canals. Scottish Canals maintains one of Scotland's longest scheduled monuments.

This beautiful shortcut continues to draw visitors to the area today.

Looking across Mòine Mhór from the Crinan Canal

Walking the Canal

There are a number of options for walking along the Crinan Canal – you can walk the whole length as a one way 3 – 4 hour walk (directions here are from Ardrishaig to Crinan). Alternatively, you can break it down into four shorter two-way sections each about 11/2 – 2 hours long. Details are given below for each section. There is a twice daily bus service between Crinan and Lochgilphead, weekdays only, which stops at Cairnbaan and Bellanoch. This service allows a one way walk along the Canal.

The following information is relevant to all sections:

Terrain: Canal towpath/footpath of fine to coarse gravel though some areas are pot holed and may be muddy when wet. The towpath also contains a few short stretches of tarmac road which are shared with vehicles

Gradient: Flat most of the way, slight gradients along lock flights

Pushchair/Wheelchair friendly: Yes but see Terrain above

Refreshments: Available at several pubs and cafes in Ardrishaig, the Cairnbaan Hotel in Cairnbaan 01546 603668 or the Crinan Hotel and Coffee Shop 01546 830261

Toilets: Nearest public toilets in Ardrishaig (north end of the car park) or in Crinan village (opposite the car park)

Cycle path: Yes but see Terrain above

Dog friendly: Yes on lead throughout

Ardrishaig to Lochgilphead (Oakfield Bridge)

Park in either of the public car parks in Ardrishaig on the seaward side of the A83 (NR 852 856) opposite the Co-operative shop.

This section has a towpath both sides of the Canal and can therefore be walked in a loop.

From the car park, follow the main road south. Just before the swing bridge, on the seaward side of the road, are the mid 19th century Canal offices, and early 19th century Canal manager's house. The road crosses the Canal next to the sea lock which is Lock number 1. The sea locks at both ends of the Canal were enlarged and improved between 1930 and 1932. The pier area, now used for exporting timber from the many commercial forests of the area, is not open to the general public.

Cross over the bridge to reach the south side of the Canal. A walk to the lighthouse at the end of the southern breakwater affords excellent views both up Loch Gilp to Lochgilphead and down the loch towards Kintyre and Arran. Cross the main road to the towpath on the south side of the Canal and walk round the basin to the information boards just before Lock 2. Continue north to Lock 3 – if the water levels are low look out for masons' marks cut into the lock chamber on the south east face. Here one can either cross the Canal and follow the pavement northwards, or continue along the road to the road bridge 300 metres further on at Lock 4. A gravel towpath begins a short distance north of this bridge on the seaward side of the Canal and continues as far as Cairnbaan. A road, then a gravelled towpath, runs along the landward side of the Canal for 2 kilometres.

Walking north out of Ardrishaig there are good views of the tidal flats at the head of Loch Gilp and the town of Lochgilphead.

Just beyond the 1 mile marker, you will come to the 'Water Waster' a building which partly houses a cleverly designed device to automatically lower the water levels of the Canal when it becomes too full. Designs were drawn up for this in 1892, and the building completed in 1895.

An information board describing its operation can be found by descending the staircase at the side of the building. Continue to Oakfield Bridge (constructed in 1871) where there is also a bridge keeper's cottage of 1800. Oakfield is an iron swing bridge, made in Glasgow in 1871, and is the oldest remaining bridge on the Canal.

From Oakfield Bridge it is only a short walk into Lochgilphead.

Lochgilphead (Oakfield Bridge) to Cairnbaan

Park east of Oakfield Bridge, over the Cuilarstich Burn, by the A83/A816 junction roundabout (NR 858 880).

Use the towpath on the seaward/Lochgilphead side of the Canal, as the path on the other side soon peters out. If only undertaking this stretch the walk is therefore there and back.

You will pass two information boards and the 2, 3 and 4 mile markers before reaching

Cairnbaan. Beside Lock 5 there is a picnic table and more information boards describing the Canal, the Cairnbaan area and some local archaeology. Cairnbaan (Gaelic – white cairn) gets its name from the Bronze Age Burial Cairn which is in the field across the road bridge.

The road bridge was installed in 1933 by the engineering firm of Sir William Arrol, which also built the Forth Railway Bridge. Across the road lies the

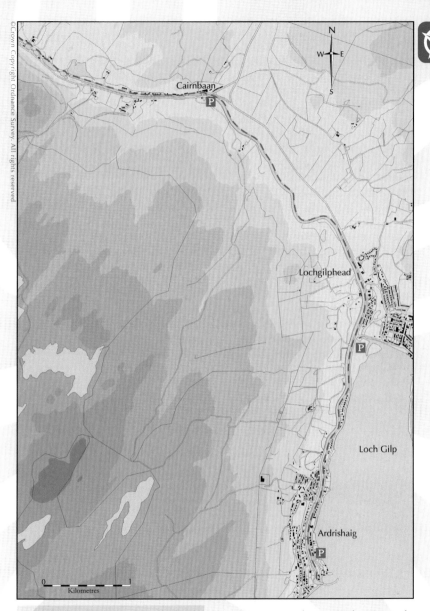

Cairnbaan Hotel, originally built in the 19th century, but modified and added to over the years. This would have accommodated travellers using the Canal.

(Here you also pass the start of walk 14 to the Cairnbaan Rock Art site).

Cairnbaan to Bellanoch

Park in one of the roadside parking bays on the southern side of the road bridge by Lock 5 (NR 838 907).

To walk this section continue on the north side of the Canal. Walk there and back on the towpath as the road on the opposite side of the Canal often has no footpath.

To continue the walk, the towpath leads to a gap in the wall, from where one can cross the main road and continue along the towpath (also a minor road) following the north side of the Canal. Passing Lock 6, you will see one of the two feeder burns which bring water into the Canal from lochs high in the Knapdale hills.

Passing Locks 7 and 8 you reach the summit level of the Canal on the stretch from Cairnbaan to Dunardry. Further along the north side of the Canal are two rows of terraced houses built around 1876 for slate quarry workers. The road becomes a track just beyond the quarriers' houses. Continuing, you pass the 5 mile marker and just before Lock 9 on the north side lies Loch a' Bharain, a lochan dammed to form an overflow for the Canal. Cross the Canal at the lock. Just below a cottage originally built to house the lock keepers you can see the remains of the Linnet shed. This now roofless building was probably originally constructed to house the passenger paddle steamer the Linnet, which was in service on the Canal between 1866 and 1929.

Cairnbaan

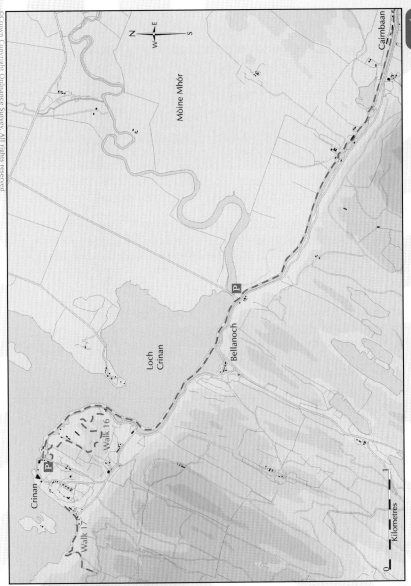

Cairnbaan

Môine Mhòr

Bellanoch

Loch Crinan

Walk 16

Walk 17

Crinan

Kilometres

Bellanoch Bay

There is a picnic table beside Lock 10 and signposts point to the walk to Dunadd (walk 10). To connect to the Near to Nature Trail (walk 15), leave the picnic area, turn left onto the road and cross to the Dunardry car park at the start of the walk. Return to the north side of the Canal and follow the towpath down to Lock 11 where there is an original lock keeper's cottage on the north side of the Canal. Next to the lock is a hand operated rolling cantilever bridge, the only one on the Canal. Having originally been used over the sea lock at Ardrishaig, this bridge was moved here in 1900 as the foundations of the lock chamber were insufficient to support the weight of a swing bridge.

Beyond Lock 11 the view across the Mòine Mhór opens out with distant views to the hills of Scarba and Mull. A level section of the Canal runs from here to Crinan. Just before the 6 mile marker there is an information board about the Mòine Mhór National Nature Reserve which lies on the north side of this part of the Canal.

Across the Moss to the north east you can see the hill of Dunadd, rising from the flat Add Basin. You now approach Bellanoch Bridge, where there is a picnic table and more information boards describing the Canal and landscape.

Bellanoch to Crinan

Park in the parking bay on the B8025 just north of Islandadd Bridge (NR 805 926).

Walk this section on the north side of the Canal. If only undertaking this stretch walk there and back as there is often no footpath on the road on the south side of the Canal.

Cross the minor road and rejoin the towpath. From here you will see the Islandadd Bridge spanning the River Add on your right. It dates from 1851 and was built by the Poltalloch Estate at the same time as the road that crosses the Mòine Mhór – the Moss Road

as it is known locally. Before the bridge was built a ferry took passengers across the estuary from Crinan Ferry to the landing just beyond Islandadd Bridge.

From Bellanoch to Crinan there are good views of the estuary where ducks, waders, swans, geese and other birds can often be seen. On the wooded bank opposite is a heronry. The 7 mile marker is passed and soon the Canal widens out into Bellanoch Bay which contains a marina. Among the 19th century buildings there is a former school and schoolhouse, recognisable by its gothic

Bellanoch Bridge

windows. Bellanoch Church, built in 1869, is on the hill behind it. Continue past the 8 mile marker to Crinan Bridge, the last swing bridge on the Canal.

Information boards by the bridge describe the Canal and Crinan Wood (walk 16). These are in the hills above the Canal and can be reached by crossing the bridge, turning left and taking the signposted footpath up through the woods. From the bridge the towpath takes you along the final section of the Canal to Crinan. Here the Canal is narrow in places as it had to be cut through many ribs of hard rock. Blasting operations left dangerous rocky projections and 11 steamers sank here between 1885 and 1921.

Across Loch Crinan, Duntrune Castle can be seen on a promontory. This is a fine medieval tower house and enclosure, which has been renovated several times in its history, most recently in the 1950s. It remains a private residence today.

Just before Crinan there is a small bridge which carries the towpath over a sluice, allowing water to drain from the Canal, just beyond which is a large pipe through which seawater can be pumped into the Canal when water is needed.

At Crinan, follow the Canal past the 8½ mile marker then round to the right as far as the hexagonal navigation lighthouse at its end. There are information boards at the Basin. Cross the Canal at Lock 14 or the Sea Lock, and explore the small picturesque village of Crinan. 'Vic 32', one of only two surviving coal fired Clyde Puffers, is often moored in the basin.

There are wonderful views across the Sound of Jura to the island of Jura, the Gulf of Corryvreckan, and Scarba. You can also see the tip of the Craignish peninsula and look northwards towards Mull.

To return, retrace your steps. There is a free car park at Crinan (NR 788 942), near the Canal, coffee shop and hotel, if you wish to leave your car at the finish.

14 CAIRNBAAN ROCK ART

Two superb, richly decorated outcrops of prehistoric rock art

Grid reference at start and finish: NR 839 907 (OS 1:50,000 sheet 55)
Distance: 0.7 miles/1.2 km
Parking at start and finish: Small informal car park on B841 in a
    roadside parking bay 100 metres west of Cairnbaan Bridge
Loop/There and back: There and back
Duration: 30 – 45 minutes
Terrain: Paths, fields
Gradient: Very steep ascent near start (and descent near finish).
    Moderate
Pushchair/Wheelchair friendly: No
Refreshments: At the Cairnbaan Hotel 01546 603668
Toilets: Nearest public toilets at Front Green, Lochgilphead
Cycle path: No
Dog friendly: On lead only

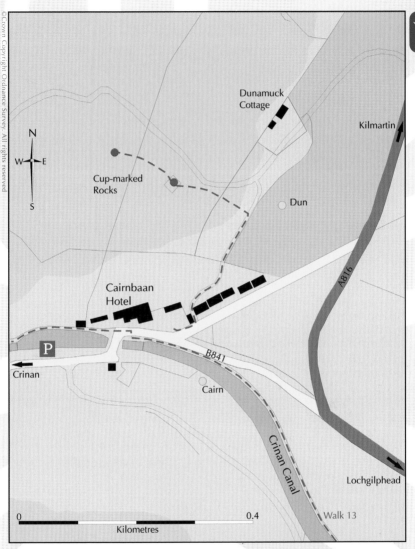

Dunamuck
Cottage

Kilmartin

N
W—E
S

Cup-marked
Rocks

Dun

A816

Cairnbaan
Hotel

P

Crinan

B841

Cairn

Crinan Canal

Lochgilphead

Walk 13

0   0.4
Kilometres

Detail of the upper panel at Cairnbaan

Cross the canal (by the swing bridge or lock gates) and the B841 road and head east for 100 metres until you see the signposted start of the walk, entitled 'Cup and Ring Marks', between the Cairnbaan Hotel and the adjacent houses. The hotel began life in the early 19th century as a staging-post inn. Look out for the triangular field that sits between the two roads leading into Cairnbaan. This was a stance for cattle being driven to and from the Kilmichael Tryst (walk 11).

Follow a fenced gravel path with the hotel on your left; the path bends right behind the houses on your right for a short distance. At the end of the fence on the right a small sign points to the 'Inscribed Rocks'. The path climbs steeply at first (but soon eases) through mature deciduous trees. Go through a kissing gate in a mossy stone wall and along a well defined path with a stone wall on your right. The surface is somewhat uneven and becomes more so a few hundred metres along where the path bends left through the trees.

There are the scant remains of a ruined dun on a natural crag on your right, but this is very difficult to access through the trees so not recommended.

About 40 metres further on, climb some stone steps to a vehicle track; bear left for a short distance to another kissing gate between the end of a stone wall and a fence post.

A grassy path crosses a field to a metal-fenced enclosure with a small stile to enable you to inspect the rock art close up. The outcrops lie on a slight rise in the landscape where there are good views to the south across the Crinan Canal and Lochgilphead.

The metal railed fence encloses three Prehistoric cup and ring marked rock outcrops.

As well as the more common cup and ring marks, the largest sheet within the fenced enclosure has several lengths of grooving. Look out for the long gutters which run downslope from several of the cups at the south end of the largest outcrop.

A small sign points to 'Other Carvings'. Cross a field for about 100 metres to a kissing gate in a stone wall and follow a grassy path, likely to be wet, for about 30 metres to the carved outcrop. The marks on this are even clearer than on the slab below.

This outcrop is one of the best examples of cup and ring marks in the area. As well as the more common cup marks, there are a number of conjoined multiple-ringed cup motifs. To the bottom right of the outcrop is an unusual motif which resembles a star, but don't be disappointed if you can't find it because it is badly weathered and very hard to see now.

There may well be more rock carvings in the vicinity, but please do not attempt to search for these as this could damage these fragile remains.

Note that there's no access beyond here. Retrace your steps to the start.

A plan of the upper panel at Cairnbaan

15 NEAR TO NATURE TRAIL, DUNARDRY

An exciting, challenging trail around Dunardry Burn

Grid reference at start and finish: NR 824 909 (OS 1:50,000 sheet 55)

Distance: 1.5 miles/2.4 km

Parking at start and finish: Forestry Commission's Dunardry car park and picnic area above the B841 Cairnbaan-Crinan road, 1.2 miles/2 km west of Cairnbaan swing bridge

Loop/There and back: Loop

Duration: 45 minutes – 1 hour

Terrain: Forest tracks, paths (some rough), steps, some very steep with exposed steep edges to the burn

Gradient: Several steep ascents and descents. Strenuous.

Pushchair/Wheelchair friendly: No

Refreshments: At the Cairnbaan Hotel 01546 603668

Toilets: Nearest public toilets at Front Green, Lochgilphead or by Crinan car park

Cycle path: No

Dog friendly: Yes

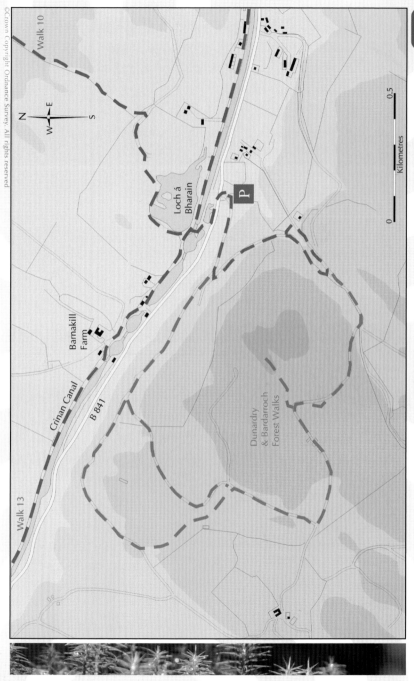

Walk 10

N

W E

S

Loch á Bharain

P

Barnakill Farm

Crinan Canal

B 841

Walk 13

Dunardry & Bardarroch Forest Walks

0.5

Kilometres

0

At the car park you'll find information boards which provide a good introduction to the walks you can do in Dunardry Forest. The Near to Nature Trail can be completed on its own, as described here, or added to a longer walk (up to 3 miles/4.8 km), following the Dunardry and/or Bardarroch Trails through the forest.

This path was created so that visitors could experience a gorge habitat, and see the rich diversity of plants that thrive in this unique environment. Look out for ferns and mosses as you cross the bridges. The burn that flows through the gorge from the reservoirs in the hills is one of a network of burns that feeds the Crinan Canal. The woodlands are part of the 'temperate rainforest' – quite common in Argyll, but very rare globally.

Walk up the wide forest track from the car park; about 200 metres after, at a disused quarry and beside an information board about Ancient Woodlands, turn left along the green and yellow waymarked path. The path is steep at the start but soon levels to a wide grassy track. At the top of the rise you reach a stone seat overlooking Cairnbaan and the Crinan Canal.

Continue until you reach a junction with a signpost 'Near to Nature.' Turn left

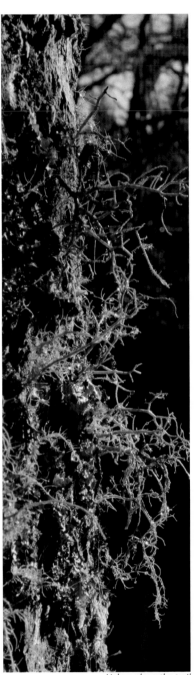

Lichen along the trail

Wintery weather on the Near to Nature trail

here and take the path and stone steps down to the burn. Cross the footbridge and turn right. Continue along the path until you reach two further footbridges that take you across the burn. Climb the very steep stone steps and footpath away from the burn until you reach an arch in a birch wall. Go through the wall and turn right up to the forest road.

Take an immediate right by the information board to rejoin the footpath down to the next bridge that crosses the burn. Cross the bridge and continue along the footpath until it reaches the junction with the other trails. Turn right here and follow the footpath, passing the right turn taken on the way out (by the Near to Nature signpost). Retrace your steps to the forest road; turn right and walk back down to the car park.

View over the Crinan Canal

16 CRINAN WOOD

A hidden Celtic rainforest

Grid reference at start and finish: NR 788 942 (OS 1:50,000 sheet 55)

Distance: 1.6 miles/2.5 km

Parking at start and finish: From the B841, follow signs to Crinan along narrow single track roads, past the prominent hotel to the clearly signposted public car park, immediately west of the sea lock in Crinan village.

Loop/There and back: Loop – there are two options for this walk, although both start and end at the same point.

Duration: 1¼ – 1½ hours

Terrain: Canal towpath, footpaths (some rough and rocky), minor roads

Gradient: Steep steps and slope at start and en route; maximum height reached – 96 metres above sea level. Moderate

Pushchair/Wheelchair friendly: No

Refreshments: At the Crinan Hotel and Coffee Shop 01546 830261

Toilets: Nearest public toilets in Crinan village (opposite the car park)

Cycle path: No

Dog friendly: Yes

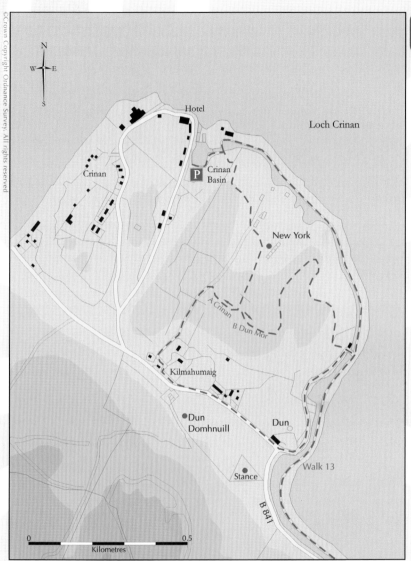

Hotel

Loch Crinan

Crinan

P Crinan Basin

New York

A Crinan
B Dun Mor

Kilmahumaig

●Dun Domhnuill

Dun

Stance

Walk 13

B 841

0   0.5
Kilometres

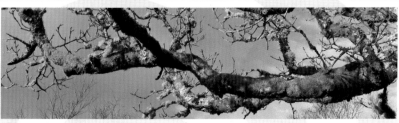

As you turn up the hill towards the car park at Crinan there is a rectangular enclosed field to your left. This is a drovers' stance, where cattle from the Islands would have been kept overnight before being driven on to the Kilmichael Tryst and the south. A bit further up the hill you will see a steep mound in the field to your left. This is called Dun Domhnuill ('Donald's Mound'), traditionally a moot hill or judgement-seat of the Lords of the Isles. It is not a dun fortification, and there has been some speculation as to its antiquity. On the opposite side of the road there is the medieval burial ground of Kilmahumaig, which is likely to have been dedicated to a Saint Colmán, sometimes spelt Colmóc.

Once at the car park in Crinan, walk along the canal towpath a short distance, step around the boom for Lock gate No 14. Beyond this is an information board about Crinan Wood. Climb the steps to your right, noting the distinctive Woodland Trust waymarker. The narrow path climbs steeply, with uneven steps in places, muddy patches and rough path edges giving way to steep drops – take care.

Descending from Dun Mor in Crinan Wood

The moist warm climate of the woodlands along the western seaboard of Scotland has led to them being called a temperate rainforest, or somewhat more romantically, a Celtic rainforest. Crinan Wood is part of a very special environment, a remnant of native woodlands that would have covered extensive areas of Scotland thousands of years ago. Although this small area of that great wood exists in some ways unchanged, there are signs that people used the trees and other plants. For example, you might spot a veteran coppiced tree on your walk through the woods.

The pure air of the west coast supports an amazing diversity of ferns, lichens and mosses. Crinan Wood has some with wonderfully descriptive names such as the golden scale fern, hay-scented fern, Tunbridge filmy fern, Wilson's filmy fern, blobby jelly lichen, golden specklebelly and Norwegian specklebelly.

Otter

Twenty four species of birds have been recorded here, including buzzard, tree creeper, redstart and wood warbler. How many did you see?

Most of the trees in the woods are native species that arrived after the last ice age. Oak and birch predominate, and there are also some hazel, ash, rowan, elm, willow, wych elm and holly, with alder growing in the boggier ground. Beech and sycamore are 19th century additions. Look out for 'phoenix trees' – these are specimens that have fallen, but retained enough roots to continue growing.

Crinan Wood has an area of heath and some open glades which were used for agriculture in earlier times. In summer you might spot the Pearl Bordered Fritillary Butterfly here, and be able to pick blaeberries.

The wood is home to red squirrel and bats. If you are very lucky, you might spot an otter close to the shore.

Red squirrel

Soon you reach a plateau dotted with rocky humps and bumps; just 10 metres to your right a short path leads to an excellent viewpoint over Loch Crinan, the Corryvreckan whirlpool and the Islands of Jura, Scarba and Mull.

The present home of the Malcolms of Poltalloch, Duntrune Castle, can be seen through the trees. This is a fine medieval tower house and enclosure, extensively renovated in the 1950s, and a private residence.

The path crosses the wooded plateau then descends steeply. At the bottom of the hill is a junction with a private access road, opposite a red roofed cottage. Turn right along this access road.

Walk along this road for about 30 metres then, following a waymarker, cross rough grass to another flight of steps up through rocks. Take care not to miss a sharp left bend at the top of the climb and promptly descend steeply, past some wonderfully moss-festooned trees, to an open grassy glen.

In the 18th century various products derived from woodlands became valuable, including charcoal for iron smelting, and bark for tannin, used in leather manufacture. Trees would have been managed by coppicing rather than felling, so that the regrowth could be harvested. The remains of the tower that you can see at Crinan Harbour was part of a works established in 1824 to produce wood acid, used in the printing industry. It is known locally as the 'Vinegar Factory'.

The woodland was acquired along with other lands by the Malcolm Family towards the end of the 18th century. After the First World War Crinan Wood passed from their ownership to the Forestry Commission. Although much of the surrounding landscape was forested with sitka spruce, this did not happen to Crinan Wood and it was acquired in 1988 by the Woodland Trust which now manages it.

On the trail through Crinan Wood

The view north from Crinan Wood

Here you turn right (as waymarked) but first, have a look at 'New York' the remains of a line of 18th or 19th century stone cottages nearby. These might have been accommodation for the workers building the Crinan Canal in the late 1700s and early 1800s. The 1860s Ordnance Survey map shows them as deserted. There is also a very badly denuded Dun in the woods.

Back to the walk: follow the grassy path up the glen, past numerous young trees planted by the Woodland Trust. Pause on the crest to take in the views of Loch Crinan to the north. Go down to a T-junction.

Here you have two options. Crinan is signed to the right. This route takes you back along the road and towpath and is fairly level throughout. To the left is a steep climb to Dun Mor – well worth the effort for the 360 degree panoramic views of the Add Estuary, Kilmartin Glen and the Sound of Jura.

View towards Kilmartin Glen from Crinan Wood

Walk A - To Crinan

Turn right at the waymarker signed Crinan and continue steeply down to an open grassy glade in which stands a Solstice marker community artwork consisting of a ring of six timber posts within which is a small, ground level stone circle (modern). A few steps further on you reach a vehicle track and an information board.

Turn left here and follow the track down past a few houses to a minor road; turn left. Walk along this road and at the sharp right hand bend take the access road to the left towards the canal. This road ends at a swing bridge across the canal; cross over and continue left along the towpath. This takes you back to Lock 14, the most convenient crossing to reach the Crinan car park.

Lichen in Crinan Wood

Walk B - To Dun Mor

Turn left at the T-junction signed Dun Mor. Follow the grassy path to the base of the hill and then continue up the steep path which has rocky steps and drops to the edge – take care. At the summit there is a large stone boulder which doubles as a convenient seat; from here you can see a panorama of the Add Estuary, Dunadd, the Mòine Mhór, Kilmartin Glen, Loch Crinan and Duntrune, the Dorus Mor and Corryvreckan, the Islands of Jura, Scarba and Mull, and Knapdale.

Continue along the grassy track down the hill, where you re-enter the natural woodland. Again there are several steep rocky stepped sections, but also several seats and viewpoints from which to enjoy the spectacular views. As you reach the bottom of the hill there is a set of steep steps that bring you back to the canal level. Turn left onto the access road and cross over the canal at the swing bridge. Turn left onto the towpath and follow this until you reach Lock 14, the most convenient crossing to the Crinan car park.

17 CASTLE DOUNIE

A Dun and spectacular sea views

Grid reference at start and finish: NR 782 940 (OS 1:50,000 sheet 55)
Distance: 3 miles/4.8 km
Parking at start and finish: Follow B841 generally northwest from
    Cairnbaan; 1.3 miles/2 km past the junction of the B8025 along
    single track road, bear left towards Crinan Harbour. Turn right at
    shoreside T-junction to a public car park 150 metres along.
Loop/There and back: Loop
Duration: 2¼ – 2½ hours
Terrain: Shoreline, narrow rocky path, steep tracks and paths, forest road
Gradient: Steep steps, paths and tracks throughout; Castle Dounie is
    approximately 170m above sea level. Strenuous
Pushchair/Wheelchair friendly: No
Refreshments: At the Crinan Hotel and Coffee Shop 01546 830261
Toilets: Nearest public toilets in Crinan village (opposite the car park)
Cycle path: Part only, along Ardnoe cycle trail
Dog friendly: Yes

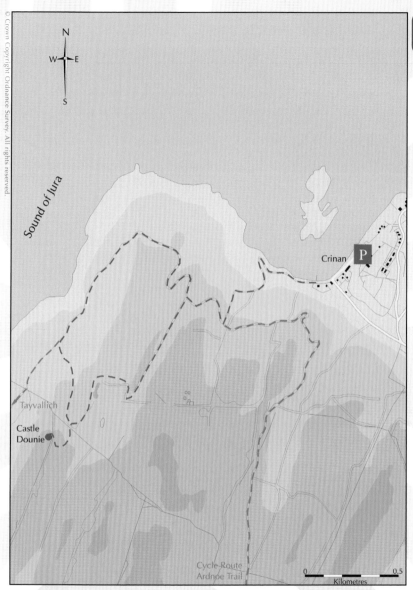

N
W E
S

Sound of Jura

Crinan P

Tayvallich

Castle
Dounie

Cycle Route
Ardnoe Trail

0   0.5
Kilometres

From the car park, where there's a Forestry Commission information board about the Crinan Trail to Castle Dounie, walk back along the minor road to a waymarker on the right. Cross a small burn and walk along the grass fringing the shingle beach, then along the shingle, which should be accessible at all but the highest tides. Continue up steps into the woodland to a good firm path through the trees parallel to the shore and past a scenically sited bench.

You will find yourself in ancient woodland which hosts an abundance of flora and fauna including various mosses, lichens & liverworts for which Argyll is famous. If you are here in spring time you will see (and smell!) patches of wild garlic as well as bluebells and many other flowers. These are followed later in the year by stands of yellow flag irises. It is worth visiting the woodland just to listen to the multitude of birds against the sound of the sea. The woods are also home to red, sika and roe deer, which you might see darting through the trees and if you are very lucky a red squirrel might just be glimpsed. Higher up on the moors, the rare black grouse has in recent years become more abundant.

The path then bends left - by the green banded waymarker you will see a narrow track on the right out to Ardnoe Point and the 'Sailor's Grave'.

The 'Sailor's Grave' has a headstone which was erected by a widow to the memory of her husband, John Black, Master of the schooner Diana, who died of cholera in 1832.

The shoreline near Crinan

Retrace your steps to the main path, which starts to gain height, soon up steps, affording lovely views of Loch Crinan, the harbour and Eilean da Mheinn just offshore. Soon you're on a wide, mainly grassy path with a bench half way up on which to rest and look out at the view. This leads into mixed forest, ascending fairly steeply but with a few level breaks.

Continue up to a wide forest road and turn right, now climbing much less steeply. Very soon you'll enjoy fine views west to the northern end of the Isle of Jura, to Scarba and Mull. About 300 metres along the track you come to a junction signposted for 'Forest Walk' to the left (and a cycle route to Carsaig to the right). Turn left here on the track which leads up a narrow wooded glen to a crest. Turn right along a waymarked, wide grassy path. This bends sharp right and descends on steps to a gravel path across a small glen. The path then goes up and over a low ridge to the seaward side of the ridge and an uninterrupted view of the Sound of Jura with a convenient picnic bench. It continues along the slope and across a slight dip to a junction. Here the waymarked route points right – to reach Castle Dounie turn left here onto a well-made path. This path twists back and forth up the Creag Mhór ridge to steps leading to the entrance to Castle Dounie right on the summit. The view is truly spectacular; myriad

islets in the Sound of Jura, the island itself sprawling across the western horizon, and chunky Scarba to its north on the far side of Corryvreckan whirlpool.

The Sound of Jura

The Corryvreckan whirlpool is the third largest in the world. Strong Atlantic currents rush through the narrow gap between Scarba and Jura, this combined with some unusual seabed geography produces the whirlpool that can at times make a very loud roaring noise.

The seas around this part of Scotland support a wealth of life, and if you are lucky you might see surfacing minke whales, basking sharks, or even a leaping dolphin.

If you have binoculars, you might also be able to spot the white farm house called Barnhill, on Jura. This is where George Orwell wrote his most famous novel, 1984.

17 CASTLE DOUNIE

As you approach Castle Dounie you will see that the most substantial section of wall, on the southern side, is visible from a dip. The site offers one of the most impressive views in Argyll along the Sound of Jura.

This site is not a typical Argyll dun as it has several distinctive features including the addition of an extra section of walling which encloses two chambers.

Look out for a large slab at the north east end of the north chamber, which might be evidence of a corbelled roof.

In the same chamber there is a small recess in the wall. A stairway might have led to the wall heads, almost certainly so the inhabitants could survey the surrounding landscape and seas.

A recent small excavation by Kilmartin Museum (commissioned by Forestry Commission Scotland), in advance of the new path, confirmed that the entrance had been modified during the life use of the dun – suggesting perhaps that it was occupied for some time.

Looking south from Castle Dounie

Sunset at Ardnoe Point

Castle Dounie from the forest road

Retrace your steps to the waymarked junction. Continue straight on to descend steeply, partly via steps, to a forest road; this is part of the Ardnoe cycle route. Turn right here. On the way down, it's worth pausing to look back for an impressive view of the pinnacle on which Castle Dounie sits. The track gains height to a crest where there are picnic tables and two Dalriada information boards. Continue until you reach the junction where you turned left on the outward journey. Continue straight on for about 300 metres to the left turn, down the steep slope to the shore of Loch Crinan and so back to the start.

BARNLUASGAN WOODS

A walk in the Celtic Rainforest, a viewpoint, a lochside path and lots of chances to see wildlife

ⓘ **Grid reference at start and finish:** NR 790 910 (OS 1:50,000 sheet 55)

Parking at start and finish: Forestry Commission car park beside junction of B8025 and Achnamara roads, 1.1 miles/1.8 km south of junction on B841 Cairnbaan-Crinan road. The small information centre here is open all year round, and contains information about the Scottish Beaver Trial as well as information about the surrounding area

Refreshments: At the Crinan Hotel and Coffee Shop 01546 830261, the Tayvallich Inn 01546 870282, or the Tayvallich Coffee Shop 01546 870281

Toilets: Nearest public toilets in Crinan village (opposite the car park), or in Tayvallich (opposite the village hall)

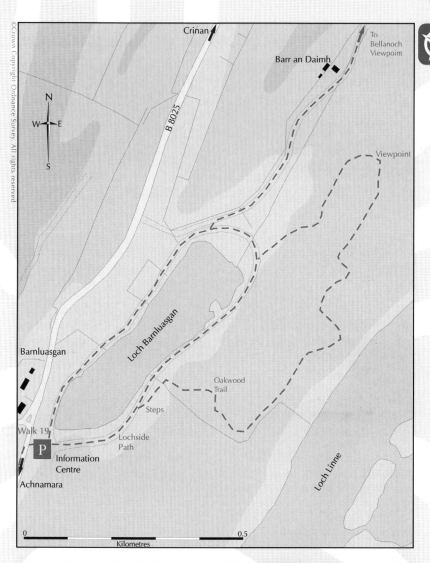

Crinan

Barr an Daimh

To Bellanoch Viewpoint

B 8025

N
W—E
S

Viewpoint

Loch Barnluasgan

Barnluasgan

Oakwood Trail

Steps

Walk 19

Lochside Path

P
Information Centre

Achnamara

Loch Linne

0   0.5
Kilometres

Along the ridge to the west of the car park there is a line of enclosures, and a Dun. The Dun was excavated by Kilmartin Museum in 2005/6. Evidence was found of Iron Age settlement including charred barley grain and a quern stone which would have been used to grind the grain into flour. Other finds were struck flint, worked stone and spindle whorls. The latter would have been used to spin wool or other materials to make thread which could have then been woven into cloth.

This ridge, and the one which Barnluasgan Woods are on, are the characteristic 'knaps' (or cnaps) of Knapdale, a word derived from Norse, meaning ridge or rise; dale or dell, being the glens between the ridges.

Formed more than 600 million years ago these distinctive ridges and glens were caused by alternating bands of hard and soft rocks; the latter being more easily eroded. They were originally deposited as near horizontal sheets and became deeply buried in the Earth's crust some 600 or so million years ago. Heat and pressure at such a depth transformed these deposits into what we now call metamorphic rock.

There are three walks starting from the car park, one of which takes you into the heart of the Atlantic oak woodlands. If you brave the steep climb up the hill

Buzzard

you will see breathtaking, ever changing views.

The woodland is known for its rich diversity of habitats, and a wealth of flora and fauna thrive here.

Aside from the beavers (see walk 19 for more information on the Beaver Trial) other mammals to look out for are red, sika and roe deer, often seen darting through the trees early in the morning or at dusk. Various species of bats can also be seen at dusk. You might catch a glimpse of a red squirrel, badger, or even a pine marten. Very rare is the Scottish wildcat, but they are thought to inhabit these woods. More easily seen are birds, so look out for longtailed, great, coal and blue tits, goldcrests, treecreepers, buzzards and jays. The lochs are also home to goldeneye ducks and whooper swans in winter and in spring it is a spawning ground for frogs and toads.

Wildlife Trail

Distance: 1 mile/1.6 km
Loop/There and back: Loop
Duration: 30 – 40 minutes
Terrain: Firm path
Gradient: Level all the way. Easy
Pushchair/Wheelchair friendly: Yes
Cycle path: Yes
Dog friendly: Yes

Along the Wildlife Trail

This all abilities path starts in the northern corner of the car park close to the road, and is signposted to the Bellanoch viewpoint. Take the short flight of stone steps, or the disabled ramp, to access the wide path which crosses the old rough grazing that fringes one side of Loch Barnluasgan. In this area in early summer you might spot an endangered butterfly, the Pearl Bordered Fritillary. 'Signal posts' provide information on the local wildlife. About 500 metres along you pass a junction where a sign points right to 'Bellanoch Viewpoint'.

Continue along the lochside path. Within 100 metres you come to a short path to the right leading to a wildlife hide.

About 50 metres on from the turnoff to the hide pass a junction with the Oakwood Trail on the left. More signal posts further on tell you about habitats, ferns and lichens, abundant in the woods. The path leads on through water tolerant alder trees on the lochside, past the junction with the other end of the Oakwood Trail, then a lochside jetty, back to the car park.

Bellanoch Viewpoint (also called Barr an Daimh Viewpoint)

Distance: 2 miles/3.2 km return; 3 miles/4.8 km with Lochside circuit
Loop/There and back: There and back
Duration: 1 hour; with Lochside circuit 1¼ - 1½ hours
Terrain: Firm path and forest road
Gradient: Level beside loch, gentle rise to lookout. Easy-moderate
Pushchair/Wheelchair friendly: Not suitable for wheelchairs
Cycle path: Yes
Dog friendly: Yes

From the junction on the Lochside path go up to a forest road and turn right to head towards the viewpoint. The young trees along the way are part of a programme to regenerate former native woodland sites in Knapdale. They have re-seeded into the area after the removal of a crop of conifers in the 1990s. There is a lot of birch here, but you will also see hazel, rowan, ash and willows. The track gains height gradually, past the Barr an Daimh Centre.

Barr an Daimh

This deserted settlement was part of the Poltalloch Estate, having been purchased at the same time as Kilmory Oib (walk 20) and Arichonan (walk 21). The woodlands were managed, but perhaps not that intensively, and this has preserved in places rare species of lichens which grow on trees.

In the 1920s/30s the land around Barr an Daimh was sold to Forestry Commission Scotland. As the open ground was planted, and oak woods were converted to conifer plantations, the settlement was used by forestry workers. In the 1990s it was leased to the Argyll Green Woodworkers Association. Over their 10 year lease of the site they repaired the 19th century cottage, reroofed the byre, and built a cruck framed shelter where woodworking and charcoal making courses were held. They also built one of the finest compost toilets (also known as the Log Loo!) in Scotland.

Soon the track reaches a crest then descends, bends left and leads on in about 150 metres to the view point. Among much else, the highlights of the view are the River Add, the Crinan Canal (walk 13) and the broad expanses of Mòine Mhór (walk 8) with Dunadd beyond (walk 9). Retrace your steps to the Lochside path to return to the start.

Lichen at Barnluasgan

Above Loch Barnluasgan

Oakwood Trail

Distance: 1.5 miles/2.4 km; with part of Lochside circuit 2.4 miles/3.9 km
Loop/There and back: Loop
Duration: 50 minutes – 1 hour; with Lochside circuit 1½ - 1¾ hours
Terrain: Firm path, steep flights of steps, narrow path, rough in places
Gradient: Level beside loch, steep ascents and descents in
     Oakwood. Moderate
Pushchair/Wheelchair friendly: No
Cycle path: No
Dog friendly: Yes

This description follows the Trail clockwise from the Lochside Path at the junction near the north-eastern corner of the loch. Steps lead up to a comparatively rough path, with green oak leaf waymarkers. You will pass through two deer gates – just push/ pull these to open and ensure they are safely closed behind you.

This area of Atlantic Hazelwoods is one of the special features of Argyll, an ancient woodland type that probably arrived in Scotland before some of the Caledonian pine woods. They are especially important for primary plants, including lichens and mosses. If you look at the hazel stems, you will see that they are covered in a wide range of these species: over 200 are found in this area alone. The graphidion lichens are smooth and blend into the bark, providing a subtle palette of silvers, greys and blacks, while the more obvious leafy lichens, such as lungwort (which looks a bit like a lung, and indeed, it was used as a cure for lung diseases), hang down from the stems. These small areas of ancient woodland are Scotland's temperate rainforest, containing species which, although relatively common in Argyll's native woodlands, are incredibly rare globally.

Birches along the Oakwood Trail

A view from the Oakwood Trail

There is a stretch of boardwalk, followed by more steps taking you steeply up to a plateau. Among birches, willow and rowan the path bends right, then left, with steps in between and on to the summit. This excellent viewpoint overlooks nearby lochans and the characteristic 'knap and dale' landscape. There are views over Loch Linne, Loch Fidhle and Loch na' Creig Mòire.

The path descends rather steeply at first then follows a sinuous and undulating route, crossing a small burn on the way, through superb oak woods, with veteran oak trees dripping in primary plants. There are a few wych elm and ash trees with glimpsed views of Loch Barnluasgan below. Eventually the path bends right, along the edge of some conifers then drops down to a succession of flights of steps, some steep, and down to the Lochside Path. Turn left to reach the car park a few hundred metres further on.

19 LOCH COILLE-BHARR

Native woodland, loch landscape and a rare chance to see beavers

Grid reference at start and finish: NR 790 910 (OS 1:50,000 sheet 55)
Distance: 3 miles/4.8 km
Parking at start and finish: Forestry Commission's Barnluasgan car park and picnic area beside B8025 road, 1.6 miles/2.6 km south-west of B841 junction. The small information centre here is open all year round.
Loop/There and back: Loop
Duration: 2 hours
Terrain: Minor road, forest tracks, paths, some rough and narrow
Gradient: Some small hillocks, otherwise generally level. Moderate
Pushchair/Wheelchair friendly: No
Refreshments: At the Crinan Hotel and Coffee Shop 01546 830261, the Tayvallich Inn 01546 870282, or the Tayvallich Coffee Shop 01546 870281
Toilets: Nearest public toilets in Crinan village (opposite the car park), or in Tayvallich (opposite the village hall)
Cycle path: No
Dog friendly: Yes, if kept under close control

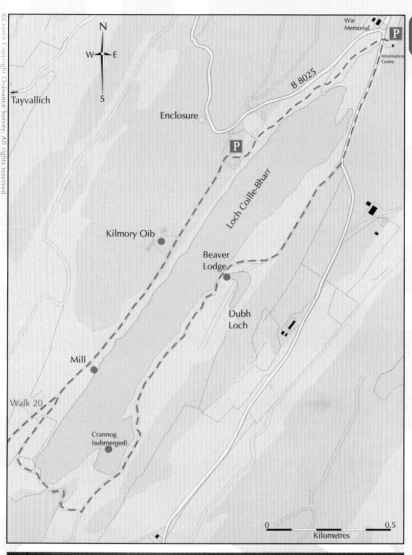

N
W—E
S

Tayvallich

Enclosure

War Memorial

P

Information Centre

B 8025

Loch Coille-Bharr

P

Kilmory Oib

Beaver Lodge

Dubh Loch

Mill

Walk 20

Crannog (submerged)

0   0.5
Kilometres

Sunset over Loch Coille-Bharr

Look out for wildlife on this walk. There are three species of deer: red, roe and the non-native sika. In the autumn time, the woods sometimes echo with the bellowing of rutting stags. At this time, you might spot a red squirrel gathering nuts to see them through the harsh winter, for the woods are full of hazel trees.

You might hear the raucous cry of a jay, or see a flash of their bright plumage through the trees. Throughout the year, but especially in autumn, look out for mushrooms and fungi, poking out from the leaf litter. There are ceps, chanterelle and many other fungi in these woods, but best not to pick them unless you are really knowledgeable because some are deadly poisonous!

The most famous inhabitant of this area of the woods is the beaver, which was reintroduced in 2009 by the Scottish Beaver Trial Project. This project is run by the Scottish Wildlife Trust (SWT), Royal Zoological Society of Scotland (RZSS) and host partners Forestry Commission Scotland. This five year trial of European beavers in Knapdale, Mid Argyll, is the first formal reintroduction of a native mammal into the wild anywhere in the UK.

Beaver Facts

The European beaver (*Castor fiber*) is an animal native to Britain, but by the 16th century they had been hunted to extinction for their thick waterproof fur. In adulthood, beavers are about the size of a large spaniel, and have a large flattened muscular tail and webbed hind feet – perfect adaptations for moving through water. Most active during dawn and dusk they live in and around freshwater lochs eating

©Jeremy Usher Smith, RZSS

A beaver family

a vegetarian diet of aquatic plants, grasses and shrubs, and woody plants in winter. Beavers live in family groups and a breeding pair can produce 2 to 4 kits each year. Generally born between April and June, having spent their first few weeks in the lodge, the kits will remain with their parents for up to two years. If beavers cannot find a suitable habitat they will sometimes create one by damming a river or stream – this also creates a habitat for other flora and fauna. The Knapdale beavers have created a dam which you can see on this walk. Their lodge is close by, but it cannot be seen as it is hidden by vegetation.

You will find more information about the beavers and the reintroduction trial in the Barnluasgan information centre, and on information boards around the walk.

Set out southwards from the Barnluasgan car park along the Achnamara road. After about 200 metres take the forest track on the right as indicated by a red-banded waymarker. There are red-banded waymarkers throughout this route. The level track leads on, round a forestry gate and then on through woodland for a few hundred yards to Dubh Loch on the left, where the beavers have built a lodge.

The path around Loch Coille-Bharr

A good firm path leads on and shortly steps up to a narrow wooded ridge above Loch Coille-Bharr. Soon you come to a viewpoint with a helpful information board and from where the beavers' dam can be seen.

Next, you cross a fairly long wide pontoon suspended over the loch, leading to steps then the onward path which winds up and down on its sinuous route.

Shortly beyond the first of several holly trees along the way you will find an information board about the beavers' lodge then a little further on, at loch level, some help with identifying beaver foot prints. A short distance beyond this you reach a wide level track. Follow it for a few hundred metres to the start of a conifer plantation on the left. Continue along the wide path. At the next junction take the stony path to the right, marked with a red-banded waymarker. This path soon ascends beside a mossy stone wall to provide views of the loch then descends to the shore. Here you will find a picnic table.

There is a crannog in this loch, however it is now submerged below the water line. One of a number of different kinds of domestic dwellings found in Scotland and Ireland, crannogs were first built during the Iron Age period, some 2,000 years ago. Generally, they consist of a wooden thatched round house built on an existing island, or an entirely artificial platform, in a loch. This kind

Loch Coille-Bharr from the viewpoint

of dwelling provided safety for the inhabitants. In 1870 divers working on the Crinan Canal were sent by a Reverend Mapleton to investigate this site – quite possibly the first underwater investigation of a crannog in Scotland. The divers found a natural island which had been built up with areas of stone revetting. They also discovered a paddle, other fragments of wood and some bone tools. The artefacts have since been lost. In later times, this crannog became known as the Minister's Stance and it was used as a fishing platform.

Evening light over the loch

From here a wider track leads down to a junction signposted for this walk and for the Faery Isles route. Turn right here and shortly you will pass a roofless stone building on the right. This is the remains of a mill – about which there is more information in this guide (walk 20).

A path up to the right here leads to a good viewpoint over Loch Coille-Bharr.

Continue along the path from the mill where you will reach the southern end of the clearing around Kilmory Oib settlement (walk 20). It's well worth the detour if you haven't been here before. There is more information on this site in walk 20. Back on the track, it's another 500 metres to the Forestry Commission's Knapdale car park.

To return to Barnluasgan car park: at the gap beside the large Forestry Commission gate, bear right by the red-banded waymarker along a narrow winding path through the forest. In the first section there is no obvious path but you quickly reach a stony path which takes you along the northern shore of Loch Coille-Bharr. Continue along the path which then descends to a gate into a field. Bear left along a wide grassy track in the field. Head to the top of the field where you will see a gate on the right; this is opposite the Barnluasgan car park at the end of the walk.

A deserted settlement, early Christian Cross, oak woods and
spectacular sea views

Grid reference at start and finish: NR 784 907 (OS 1:50,000 sheet 55)

Distance: 6 miles/10 km

Parking at start and finish: Forestry Commission's Knapdale car park
and picnic area beside the B8025 road 1.6 miles/2.6 km south
west of B841 junction

Loop/There and back: There and back

Duration: 2½ – 2¾ hours

Terrain: Forest road

Gradient: Some short ups and downs. Moderate

Pushchair/Wheelchair friendly: Not suitable for wheelchairs

Refreshments: At the Crinan Hotel and Coffee Shop 01546 830261,
the Tayvallich Inn 01546 870282, or the Tayvallich Coffee Shop
01546 870281

Toilets: Nearest public toilets in Crinan village (opposite the car
park), or in Tayvallich (opposite the village hall)

Cycle path: Yes

Dog friendly: Yes but must be on lead through southern section of walk

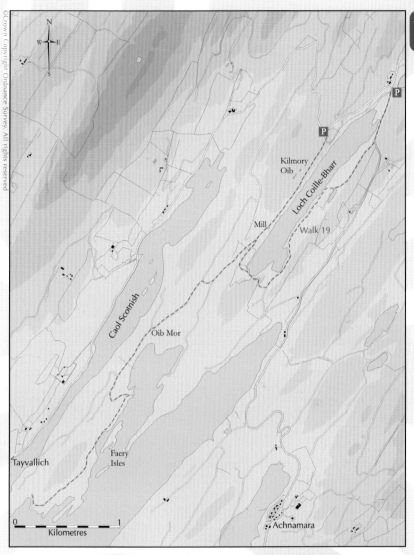

N
W E
S

P

Kilmory
Oib

Loch Coille-Bharr

Mill

Walk 19

Caol Scotnish

Oib Mor

Faery
Isles

Tayvallich

0   1
Kilometres

Achnamara

The view south across Loch Sween

Set out from the car park along the wide, clearly signposted, forest track. Within 500 metres you come to a clearing on the right, the deserted settlement of Kilmory Oib. There is an information board on the edge of the surrounding forest beside the grassy path leading towards the stone buildings, with a reconstruction of what the site might have looked like when it was inhabited.

Kilmory Oib Deserted Township

Kilmory Oib is one of a number of deserted settlement sites in North Knapdale. Others include Arichonan (walk 21), and Barr an Daimh (walk 18). A feature which sets this site apart is the early medieval carved stone. Although heavily worn now, a complex series of motifs are just visible; there is a cross on both sides and one face bears an image of birds and animals, as well as discs interpreted as the sun and moon. The stone dates from the 8th or 9th century, and stands next to a 'holy well'.

This stone, and the 'Kil' element in the place name, suggests there was an early ecclesiastical presence at the site around the time the cross was carved. Few sites of this kind have been excavated previously, so speculation that they may be medieval in origin can't be confirmed. With this in mind, following a survey, Kilmartin Museum conducted a small scale excavation of the site in 2008. Although there was evidence of an earlier post built structure, most of the material found dated to the 19th century.

Kilmory Oib

Close by is Achadh na Cille Oib. Little remains of this burial ground today, and many of the carved medieval stones have been moved. Most are in Kelvingrove Museum, but one now stands in St Columba's Episcopal Church on the Poltalloch Estate, and it was probably moved around the time the church was built in the mid 19th century. This led to speculation that the stone at the well had been moved to Kilmory Oib around the same time, and it is even possible that the name itself moved. Perhaps there never was a chapel on this site?

There are 17 buildings here, including houses and byres, some of which have been altered over time. There are two circular mounds of rubble which might be corn drying kilns. People would have been tenant farmers, working the land in the same way as the people living at the nearby settlement of Arichonan (walk 21). Most of the standing ruined buildings date to the late 18th to early 19th century. The 1851 census lists 6 households and 32 inhabitants. By this time Kilmory Oib was part of the Oib Estate, which in turn had been purchased by the Malcolm Family of Poltalloch.

Arichonan became notorious because tenants refused to comply with eviction orders. People from the surrounding communities, including this township, joined them in protest. Court documents relating to the disturbance name people who are listed as living at Kilmory Oib on the 1851 census. Kilmory Oib is not mentioned in the 1861 census, and by the 1st edition Ordnance Survey map, based on a survey of 1864, the village is shown as unroofed. By the 2nd edition Ordnance Survey, mapped in 1900, a small roofed structure is shown, occupied according to the 1901 census by Catherine Blue. She is likely to have been the last person to live here. Seven years later, in 1909, the cottage was photographed – it has no roof. Kilmory Oib had been abandoned.

As you wander around the site, look out for the distinctive triangular shaped 'windows' in one of the barns – these are vents to allow air to circulate. Close by, there is a sheep fank, built at the time the area had been converted to sheep.

In the 1930s, the Forestry Commission purchased much of Knapdale, including Kilmory Oib, and the area was planted with conifers, although much of the forest is now being restored to native woodland.

The path, which can be boggy after rain, takes you into the heart of the village. Near the far/south western end of the village, where the path bends left to rejoin the forest track, you will find the carved slab and well.

Continue along the forest track, and after 500 metres pass a tall roofless stone structure on the left, which is a ruined mill.

The Mill

Water was taken from the loch to power the mill wheels which ground grain. The lade flows down the hill close to the path. Do not go inside the building, as it is quite dangerous now. Note the arched entrance which would have accommodated the water-wheel, and you might just be able to spot reddening on the walls of the chamber to the south of the building. This was caused by fire from a kiln, used to dry grain before it was milled.

The presence of a meal mill at 'Coilebar' is documented as early as 1490. This is probably a reference to a building on this site, and it was almost certainly constructed to be used by the inhabitants of the Oib Peninsula, but by 1857 it is noted as being almost in ruins. It is mentioned in a local saying:

Tri sgoid Chnapdail
(The three boasts of Knapdale)
Carridh Loch Chrinan
(The fish cruives of Loch Crinan)
Frith ghlinn a'Bhacain
(The deer forest of Bacan's glen)
Is muileann dubh Choillebar
(And the dark mill of Coille-Bharr)

There is a 17th century story associated with the mill concerning the wife of Lachlan 'Cattanach' MacLean of Duart. He left his wife to drown on a tidal rock off the south end of Lismore – a place known as 'Lady's Rock'. MacLean was said to be angry because she had not yet produced him a son. The wife was rescued by some Knapdale fishermen and taken to Inveraray Castle. The mill and all its privileges were awarded to the rescuers.

A short distance further on you come to the junction with the Loch Coille-Bharr walk (an optional extension of this walk; see walk 19).

The forest road soon emerges into the open and in a few hundred metres turn right at a junction then left less than 100 metres further on, into fairly dense conifers. Just before you emerge from the conifers, you might see some ruined buildings either side of the track. These are the remains of Oib Mor, a township similar to Kilmory Oib – abandoned in the later half of the 19th century. The conifers soon give way to birch woodland on both sides of the track, so you may glimpse views of Loch Coille-Bharr and the long inlet of Caol Scotnish. Pass a track junction on the right and about 200 metres further on you come to a gate. Dogs must be on a lead from this point onwards as there are Highland cattle, introduced to promote forest regeneration.

Continue down the track, past an old quarry on the left, and down to the shore of an inlet from Loch Sween, where the low, partly wooded Faery Isles come into view.

The Faery Isles are an enchanting place. The surrounding ancient oak woodlands are rich in lichens and bryophytes. At low tide you can cross over to the nearest island to explore. At high tide these Atlantic woodlands really do reach right to the Atlantic, creating a seamless junction between woodland and sea. In spring watch out for the narrow leaved helleborine, a white flowered orchid. Also keep an eye out for ospreys, which nest and fish in these parts.

The track wanders up and down, passing some fine specimens of tall Scots pines. Approximately 1.4 miles/2.2km from the gate, you reach the end of the path where you will find a picnic table with a superb view south across Loch Sween. There is a short path to the right which takes you down to a very sheltered beach where you could cool off on a hot summer day.

Simply retrace your steps back to the start, enjoying even better views than on the outward journey.

Along the trail to the Faery Isles

21 ARICHONAN

A well-preserved 18th and 19th century clearance township

Grid reference at start and finish: NR 777 911 (OS 1:50,000 sheet 55)
Distance: 1.2 miles/2 km (Alternative route: 2.4 miles/4 km)
Parking at start and finish: Forestry Commission Gleann a Gealbhan
    car park beside B8025 road, 2.6 miles/4.2 km southwest of
    junction with B841 Cairnbaan-Crinan road and 1.5 miles
    southwest of the junction of the Tayvallich and Achnamara roads.
Loop/There and back: There and back
Duration: 1 hour
Terrain: Paths
Gradient: Fairly steady ascent and descent on return. Moderate
Pushchair/Wheelchair friendly: No
Refreshments: At the Crinan Hotel and Coffee Shop 01546 830261,
    the Tayvallich Inn 01546 870282, or the Tayvallich Coffee Shop
    01546 870281
Toilets: Nearest public toilets in Crinan village (opposite the car
    park), or in Tayvallich (opposite the village hall)
Cycle path: No
Dog friendly: Yes

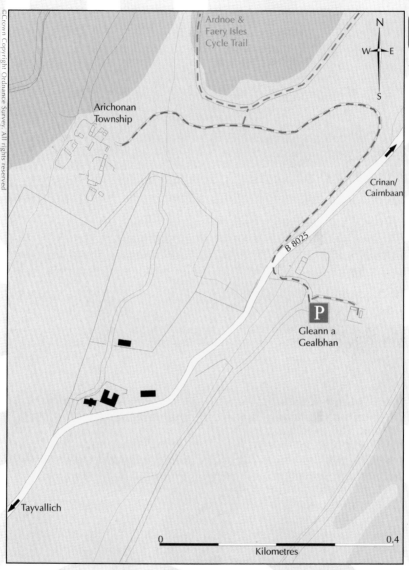

Ardnoe &
Faery Isles
Cycle Trail

Arichonan
Township

Crinan/
Cairnbaan

B 8025

P

Gleann a
Gealbhan

Tayvallich

0   0.4

Kilometres

Detail of walling at Arichonan

Just beside the car park, as you walk up the track to the main road, are the remains of the old mill and drovers' inn, which are now represented by low walls. This was part of the settlement at Glenn a Gealbhan. Other buildings can be reached by following a short path leading from the north west corner of the car park, one of which has been used as an art installation by NVA, an Edinburgh based arts organisation.

To reach Arichonan from the car park walk up the access track and cross the road with care to the yellow-banded waymarked start of a wide path. Initially it parallels the road through tall conifers then gradually bends to the left to a junction marked with another yellow-banded waymarker. Take the left path into the open clearing and then follow the grassy path to the left. The path then veers away to the right into the forest. As it contours the steep slope, you may glimpse views through the trees to Caol Scotnish. Pass a flight of steps on the right. A bridge with a stone lintel takes you across a burn and the path emerges into the open with the extensive remains of Arichonan village spread out before you. As you will see, there are good views across the waters of Caol Scotnish.

The name Arichonan means 'Chonainn's Pasture' in Gaelic, and there has been a township on this site since at least the 16th century. Like so many other settlements in the area the site is now in ruins, having been deserted for about 150 years. Some sites were gradually abandoned, but others, like Arichonan, were cleared because the landowners wished to use their land for other purposes.

By the early 17th century, the settlement and the land around it was part of the Oib Estate. In 1801 the estate was purchased by the Malcolm family and the land became part of the Poltalloch Estate. At this time there were four tenants, working 332 acres, over 50 of which were arable.

The inhabitants held the land under what was known as a 'multiple tenancy'. Families shared the land – annually allotting use of the arable land, divided into strips known as 'rigs'.

The level area in front of the township is all that remains of the strip-fields used by the tenants for growing oats, barley and potatoes. Some houses had small gardens, known as kail yards, used for growing vegetables.

Although fish would have formed part of the diet, cattle

Arichonan

were the mainstay of the economy. During the summer, cattle would be taken to graze the hill pastures and people stayed in small stone and turf huts, known as sheilings, making cheese from the milk surplus. Joined by families from nearby settlements, this would also have been time for socialising and having fun. The sheilings of Arichonan have not been identified, but the remains of hundreds of similar settlements have been recorded all over mid Argyll.

Towards the end of the 18th century, the Malcolms of Poltalloch invested in large scale agricultural improvements. Shortly after the township was purchased estate records note the houses were 'not built right at first'. The landowners' obligations to their tenants included the repair of buildings, and, at this time, some houses at Arichonan were improved. Stout slate roofs replaced thatch and others were rebuilt. The stones that project from some buildings were used to secure thatch ropes, evidence of these earlier roofs. Wooden cruck frames were used to hold up the roof beams and inside some of the houses you can see slots in the walls which indicate the former location of these frames.

On the north west terrace you will see a winnowing barn where grain was threshed. The building's use is clearly identified by the opposing doors that allowed air to pass through the building. The date 1833 is carved on the door lintel. Look out for the triangular windows in the barn serving as air vents

Walls at Arichonan

to keep stored crops and hay well aired. This type of barn window construction is typical of Argyll and can also be seen at Kilmory Oib (walk 20).

Across the track you will see the well where everyone would have hauled water.

By the mid 19th century the old system of multiple tenancy farming was giving way to new ways and cattle were being replaced by sheep. As landowners all over Scotland converted tracts of land for sheep, many people chose to leave to seek a new life abroad. Others had little choice since they had lost their homes. From Mid Argyll many folk went to Canada or Australia, or to less far flung places like Glasgow.

At Arichonan tenants were unable to pay their rent, and eventually eviction or removal notices were served for the leases to be terminated.

'.... flit and Remove themselves, their Wives, Bairns, Families, Servants, Subtenants, Cottars, Dependants, goods and gear....'

Records from 1848 show that there were 40 people living at the site. Eviction orders were ignored twice and so the estate factor William Martin decided to act. Some believe he overreacted because the Laird was away at the time. A group of 30 men from the estate were assembled, backed up by the constabulary and the Sheriff Officer who went to serve the final eviction order. They were met by a large crowd of about 200 men and women, many of whom had come from surrounding settlements in support of their neighbours. As the evictors were driven off they managed to seize a few of the protestors. Local men were asked to mediate and the prisoners were released. Support for the families at Arichonan was widespread and people living in nearby Lochgilphead came out in protest – the authorities feared a riot. A plea for troops was sent to Edinburgh, but events there prevented the dispatch of soldiers. Eventually tempers cooled, but there were recriminations. Thirteen people were accused. Five were sentenced to terms of between 4 to 8 months in prison, and served their time in Inveraray Jail, which still holds the court records of their case.

The name of one of those involved in the affray, Neil MacMillan, is carved on the cornerstone of his house, on the north west terrace.

Eventually, the families of the township resigned themselves to having to leave. Some departed for Canada, refusing the Malcolm family's offer of land in Australia.

But Arichonan did not become completely deserted. Following the departure of the tenants, one cottage was rebuilt for the shepherd who looked after the sheep grazing the former tenants' land. A large sheep fank (enclosure) was built which you will see in the middle terrace. Next to it is the two storey shepherd's house built after 1848. But eventually even the sheep left. In the 1930s the land was sold to the Forestry Commission, the hill ground was planted with trees, and the shepherd's house abandoned.

Moss on the stones of Arichonan

To return retrace your steps to the car park.

Oakwoods and loch shores – a wildlife haven

All three walks – Woodland Trail, Coastal Trail, Barr Mór Trail – start at the same point:

Grid reference at start and finish: NR 737 852 (OS 1:50,000 sheet 62)

Parking at start and finish: Follow B8025 from B841 Cairnbaan-Crinan road; bear right at a junction after 1.1 miles/1.8 km and continue along the mostly single track road to Tayvallich (further 4 miles/6.5 km). Drive through the village to a junction by the village hall; turn left for Taynish National Nature Reserve as signposted. This narrow single track road, rough in places, leads 1.2 miles/2 km to a small car park signed for the Reserve.

Refreshments: At the Tayvallich Inn 01546 870282 or the Tayvallich Coffee Shop 01546 870281

Toilets: Nearest public toilets in Tayvallich (opposite the village hall)

Dog friendly: Yes, under close control throughout

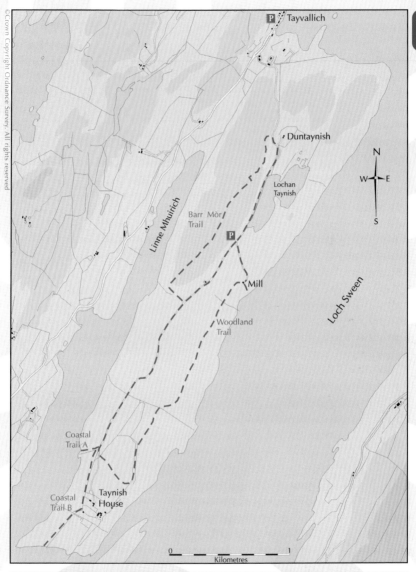

Tayvallich

Duntaynish

Lochan Taynish

Linne Mhuirich

Barr Mòr Trail

Mill

Woodland Trail

Loch Sween

Coastal Trail A

Coastal Trail B

Taynish House

N
W–E
S

0   Kilometres   1

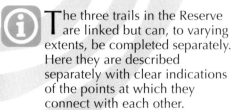

The three trails in the Reserve are linked but can, to varying extents, be completed separately. Here they are described separately with clear indications of the points at which they connect with each other.

One of the reasons Taynish is special is because it is one of the few places in Scotland where oak woods cloak the steep hills that fall down to the sea, supporting a diversity of habitats and a wealth of wildlife and plant life. Another very important feature of these temperate rainforests is the wide range of mosses, liverworts and lichens that can be found here throughout the year. There are over 400 types of lichen, ranging from the relatively common old man's beard to the far rarer yellow specklebelly. Buzzards can almost always be seen, and, if you are lucky, you might just spot (or hear) a great spotted woodpecker, or even an otter – look out to sea for a sleek head breaking the water. In the spring, the woods are carpeted by wild Scottish bluebells and the delicate white heads of wild garlic, which you are sure to smell, perhaps before you see it! In late spring, the yellow heads of flag iris carpet the fringes of boggy areas and, during the summer months, the speckled wood butterfly can be seen, along with 19 other varieties. In the autumn, as the leaves of the trees begin to change to a vibrant autumn display of colours, you might even spot the webs where the Marsh Fritillary butterfly lays its eggs.

Although humans appear to have had little impact on the woods at Taynish, a closer look reveals their presence in the form of charcoal burning platforms. Charcoal was a valuable commodity in the late 18th and early 19th centuries. For this reason, the woods would have been protected and managed. Today, they are managed by Scottish Natural Heritage.

Linne Mhuirich from the Coastal Trail

Woodland Trail

Distance: 3.1 miles/5 km
Loop/There and back: Loop
Duration: 1½ - 2 hours
Terrain: Well made path for 0.4 miles/0.7 km to Taynish Mill and picnic area; then a narrower path, rocky in places, mostly gravelled but some boggy bits; some steps; short sections across potentially boggy fields; firm vehicle track
Gradient: 1:12 gradient to/from Taynish Mill; undulating through woodland; minor ups and downs elsewhere. Moderate
Pushchair/Wheelchair friendly: To Taynish Mill only; from car park to junction with Coastal Trails
Cycle path: Only from car park 1.2 miles/2 km from car park to junction with Coastal Trails; bike racks opposite nearby sheds

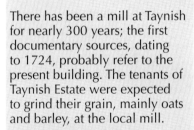

Follow the yellow oak leaf waymarked path southwards from the car park through woodland, as signposted to Taynish Mill and the shore. Soon you come to the start of the steep winding descent to the mill and picnic area. An information board fills you in on the mill's history.

On the shore at Taynish Mill

Taynish Mill

There has been a mill at Taynish for nearly 300 years; the first documentary sources, dating to 1724, probably refer to the present building. The tenants of Taynish Estate were expected to grind their grain, mainly oats and barley, at the local mill.

Documents of 1867 mention the mill in operation, but by around 1886 it is described as having gone out of use. The building had two storeys but only the lower now survives. Look out for the remains of the corn drying kiln and the wheel pit. The mill was fed by a dam and culvert leading from Lochan Taynish.

A short signposted path takes you to viewpoints on the shore of Loch Sween – a good place for spotting seabirds and waders.

Return to the picnic area and continue across a small footbridge and up past the mill (where you can see the position of the mill wheel) and a small waterfall. Steps lead up to a narrow undulating path through the oak wood at the base of low cliffs. After about 1 km the path rises to the edge of the plateau above then wanders up and down, past point W5 (Northern Rainforest) then gains the crest of the plateau at a gate through a substantial stone wall. A good level path leads on past point W4 (Boundary Wall). Then, as you pass through a lower stone wall and start to descend, there are good long views southwards across Loch Sween.

After a few minutes you'll come to a viewpoint on the left; go right here, through a gate in the fence to cross the field (where cattle may be grazing), guided by a waymarker post ahead. Cross a small burn, pass information point W3 (Pease's Field) and go down to meet a vehicle track. Turn right through a gate along the track. About 100 metres further on, pass the start of the Coastal Trails.

The Woodland Trail follows the vehicle track through woodland; information point W2 (Drovers Gate/Taynish Farm boundary) is on the far side of a gateway in the stone wall. Soon, steep-sided Barr Mór looms directly ahead and you come to the waymarked turn off to the left for the Barr Mór Trail. About 200 metres further on, pass the Gate House (point W1) which is still occupied, from where it's only 400 metres back to the start.

On the Woodland trail

Coastal Trails – Walk A and Walk B

Distances: Walk A – 150 metres; Walk B - 0.6 miles/1 km
Loop/There and back: There and back
Duration: Walk A – 10-15 minutes; Walk B – 30 minutes
Terrain: Firm path, then field path, potentially boggy, duckboards on
Walk A which can be slippery when wet
Gradient: Level. Easy
Pushchair/Wheelchair friendly: Yes – although care needs to be
taken when crossing the field
Cycle path: Cycles can be left in racks opposite sheds near the start
of the Coastal Trails

To reach the start of both of the Coastal Trails from the main Taynish car park, follow the Woodland Trail's yellow oak leaf waymarkers along the broad track leading south westwards. Soon you'll pass the Gate House, then the turnoff to the Barr Mór Trail on the right. Nearly 1.5 km beyond this point, just past some sheds on the right, and beside a field, blue wave waymarkers indicate the start of the Coastal Trails.

Walk A – take the path to the right which bends across the field to a firmer section just before a gate. Pass through

At the Piggery

the gate beyond which is a duckboard path to reach the shore. There's a picnic table nearby to the right. Return to the start by the same route.

Walk B – Continue straight ahead on the main path. Off to the left is the gate to the field, through which you would continue along the Woodland Trial. Continue on the path and soon you'll enjoy lovely views across Linne Mhuirich to the right. Continue past a stone wall and gate on the left; there is a sign to the left pointing to the Piggery. This may sound uninviting, but this restored (though roofless) 19th century stone building is now used for occasional exhibitions. Return to the main path, turn left and continue along the soft informal path that leads to the shore. Here you overlook rapids between the Taynish peninsula and the low-lying Ulva and Danna. This is a great place for seabirds and waders, and you might even spot an otter. To return retrace your steps to the start.

Barr Mór Trail

Distance: 2 miles/3 km
Loop/There and back: Loop
Duration: 1 – 1 ¼ hours
Terrain: Minor road, vehicle track; narrow path with many steep steps
Gradient: Almost level along road and track; climb to maximum height of 126 metres. Strenuous
Pushchair/Wheelchair friendly: No
Cycle path: No

Walk south west from the car park, following red eagle waymarkers (this is also part of the Woodland Trail). About 400 metres along, you pass the Gate House on the right (still occupied) and an area of bog on the left.

Another 200 metres brings you to the waymarked junction where you turn right across open moorland, where peat was once cut for fuel. (The Woodland Trail continues straight on). The path leads into woodland and immediately starts to climb. It bends right and gains height quickly as it switches back and forth across the wooded slope. The next marked feature on the ascent is a charcoal platform.

The gradient eases once you reach Barr Mór's summit plateau. A bench is well placed on the summit, a wonderful lookout for views east across Loch Sween and west to the Isles of Jura and Mull. To the south you can see Taynish House.

Continue along the open, undulating ridge and up to the northern summit which affords a particularly good view of Caol Scotnish to the north.

Charcoal platform

This platform has been cut into the hillside and drystone walling built at the front. When this site was excavated in 2003 rich deposits of charcoal were found, as well as an area of burning. So it would appear that this is where wood was burned to make charcoal, probably during the late 18th to early 19th centuries, when we know these woods were leased to the Bonawe Iron Furnace. The charcoal would have been shipped to Bonawe by sea to be used for iron smelting, a process that required vast amounts of fuel.

Over sixty similar sites are known on this peninsula. Some were excavated in the 1970s, and the excavator speculated these might have been platforms where houses were built because no charcoal was found.

Along the Barr Mór trail

The descent starts abruptly, and almost immediately Tayvallich comes into view below. Negotiate the steep and uneven steps down through oak woodland; the path leads on to the access road about 100 metres north of the entrance to Duntaynish House (which is private). Turn right to return to the car park, 1 km further on, passing secluded Lochan Taynish on the way.

Medieval grave slabs and an unusual 'Celtic' cross

Grid reference at start and finish: NR 694 805 (OS 1:50,000 sheet 55)
Distance: 0.3 miles/0.5 km
Parking at start and finish: Follow B8025 single track road southwest from B841 junction at Bellanoch, through village of Tayvallich (5 miles/8 km). Continue through the village and once out of Tayvallich continue on the road for a further 5 miles/ 8 km to the end of the public road. Go through the gate at the end of the road and park 100 metres further on along the vehicle track, in a small area on the left.
Loop/There and back: There and back
Duration: 15 – 20 minutes
Terrain: Track and paths – narrow, slightly rough up to the chapel
Gradient: Minimal. Easy
Pushchair/Wheelchair friendly: No
Refreshments: At the Tayvallich Inn 01546 870282 or the Tayvallich Coffee Shop 01546 870281
Toilets: Nearest public toilets in Tayvallich (opposite the village hall)
Cycle path: No
Dog friendly: On lead only

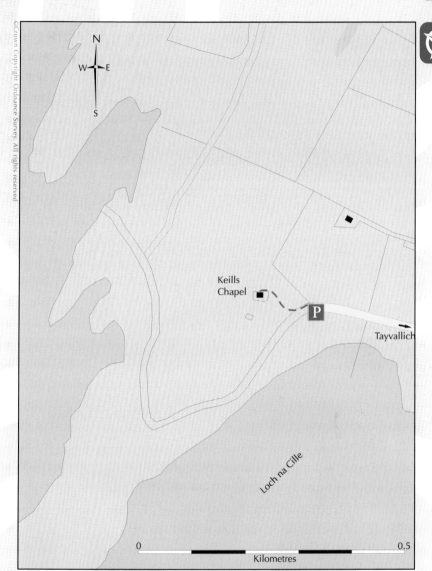

Keills
Chapel

P

Tayvallich

Loch na Cille

0   Kilometres   0.5

Detail of the Keills Cross

Walk along the vehicle track (which leads to Keills jetty) from the car park.

 In the 18th and 19th centuries, Keills was a busy port where cattle from the Islands of Islay, Jura and Colonsay were landed, and from here were driven to the markets in the south.

 As you walk along this track the chapel comes into view up on the right. A narrow un-signposted path climbs the grassy slope to the entrance to the graveyard surrounding the chapel.

 This medieval Church was once the Church of the Parish of Knapdale. From the site you can look out over Loch Sween to Castle Sween (walk 24) and to the south west to Eilean Mór (big or great island), one of the MacCormac Islands, on which a medieval chapel also stands. Both chapels are dedicated to the same Irish saint, Abbán moccu Corbmaic (sometimes recorded in documents as Cill Mhic Charmaig).

The building itself is thought to date to the later part of the 12th century, so is earlier than its dependent chapel at Kilmory (walk 25).

It was used as the parish Church for perhaps 500 years until it went out of use in the late 1600s when the parish was subdivided. It was re-roofed in the 1970s to house and protect the fine collection of carved crosses and grave slabs. The remaining walls stand today much as they did. Look out for the broken quern stones reused in their construction.

The door is always unlocked; enter through the rebuilt doorway. Inside there's more information.

Keills Church

Inside the chapel the west window remains relatively unaltered, unlike the east window. An altar would have stood at the east end, and you can still see the two aumbries (recesses or cupboards) where the tools used in services were stored.

Numerous burials have been made inside the Church (the cause of some complaint in 1649 as this was contrary to an Act of the General Assembly of the Church of Scotland).

Of the carved stones, the largest and most elaborate is the late 8th or early 9th century Keills Cross. Originally outside (a replica now stands outside in its place), the date of this monument, as well as the 'Kil' element in the place name indicate an early foundation and one of some importance at that. Abbán moccu Corbmaic is thought to have been active in the late 6th and early 7th centuries AD, so it is likely that the existing building replaced an earlier one.

Other early crosses are arranged around the walls starting from the left as you enter. There are lots of gravestones to explore too. Look out for the figure holding a book in his left hand. Writing and producing books would have been mostly an ecclesiastical preserve. Other stones date from the medieval period and are carved with motifs usual to West Highland grave slabs (see also walk 25 for more information). Look out for the harp (clàrsach or cláirseach) which is similar to an instrument in the National Museum of Scotland, itself one of only three surviving medieval Gaelic harps.

See if you can spot the small carved salmon close to the sword blade on one of the stones, which dates to the 15th century. Salmon would have been an important food source.

The wall at Keills Church

Outside, the wall is a 19th century construction. There are several unusual grave slabs in the burial ground. To visit the replica of the Keills Cross, just above the site, follow a path on the outside of the north wall of the burial ground.

Retrace your steps to the car park.

Grid reference at start and finish: NR 717 787 (OS 1:50,000 sheet 62)

Distance: 1 mile/1.6 km

Parking at start and finish: Limited parking available in a roadside parking bay, by the public telephone box, and opposite the entrance to Castle Sween Caravan Park 10.5 miles south of the junction with B8025 road.

Loop/There and back: There and back

Duration: 1 hour including time to look around the castle

Terrain: Road, footpaths, grass

Gradient: Gentle grade on access road, slight rise to castle. Easy-moderate

Pushchair/Wheelchair friendly: Yes, as far as steps to castle interior

Refreshments: At the Crinan Hotel and Coffee Shop 01546 830261, the Tayvallich Inn 01546 870282, or the Tayvallich Coffee Shop 01546 870281

Toilets: Nearest public toilets in Crinan village (opposite the car park), or in Tayvallich (opposite the village hall)

Cycle path: No

Dog friendly: On lead only

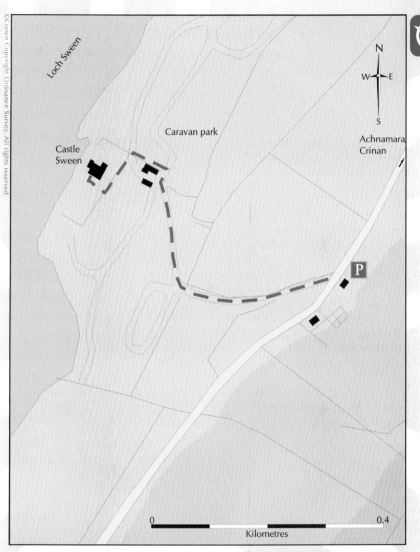

Loch Sween

Caravan park

Castle
Sween

Achnamara
Crinan

N
W — E
S

P

0   0.4
Kilometres

The shoreline at Castle Sween

From the clearly marked roadside car park, walk down the caravan park access road along the tree-lined avenue. Please DO NOT attempt to drive down into the caravan park – there is no vehicle access for castle visitors. At the bottom of the drive follow the access road around to the right – this road leads around the Shop and Restaurant for the Caravan Park (for site users only) to the castle. Walk through the access gate in the stone wall surrounding the castle.

As you walk up to the walls of the castle, look out on the left hand side for an opening in the stone. This is the bottom of a chute – this is a garderobe, (medieval toilet - use your imagination to figure out how it worked!).

The main entrance to Castle Sween is up to your left.

The castle was begun in the 12th century, and was used for probably four hundred years before falling into ruin. As with most buildings of this age what you see today is an amalgamation of many modifications and additions. The siting is well chosen, guarding the entrance to Loch Sween. In earlier times fortifications were built higher up and there is a string of Duns along the ridges you can see to the landward side. Evidently the 12th century builders had their reasons for choosing this site, for although it is on quite low ground it would have been easily defendable, and access to the sea was probably a priority. In any case the thick curtain walls, which are thought to be the earliest part of the castle, would have protected its inhabitants. It would have been a major task to level the ground and

Loch Sween and Castle Sween

bedrock to build them, as the rocks rise to almost vertical pinnacles in places. The construction of the castle is thought to have been under the orders of Suibhne; and it is from him that the family name MacSween is derived.

The entrance into Castle Sween

Walk up the steps, through the arched entrance and into the courtyard.

On your right (south east), the tower noted from outside is labelled 'south latrine tower' – this was the chute you saw from outside.

In the top right corner (north east) is the circular well – this has been cut into the bedrock, and is about 5 metres deep, supplying the whole castle with water.

Near the well are the foundations of 15th century buildings.

From the courtyard go past the well and through the entrance in the wall to steps leading down into the north east range. This is known as MacMillan's tower. Alexander MacMillan was keeper of the castle for the Lords of the Isles in the 1470s. He commissioned the MacMillan Cross, which can be seen in Kilmory Chapel (walk 25).

This tower would have had three floors, the lowest being the kitchen, which is the best preserved. There are various features to spot here, including a bread oven, a water inlet and there is also a scar where the fireplace would have once stood. Look out also for the two lancet windows dating to the 13th century, which have been incorporated into the kitchen walls. Against the wall there are three stones, one of which is half of a rotary quern, used for grinding grain. The others might be saddle querns. If so, they were made thousands of years before the castle, but they might have been used as troughs for food preparation. Feeding all the people living in the castle at this time would have been a major endeavour, and the kitchen would have been a place of great activity, noise, heat and smoke. The roof would have been made of stone, and barrel vaulted, and there were two floors of accommodation above.

Castle Sween

As you walk along past the courtyard walls, you will be passing where the great hall once stood.

Retrace your steps into the courtyard through the postern gate (secondary, often concealed entrance) and explore the north west tower. This is earlier than MacMillan's tower and dates to early in the 13th century, when a small wing was built on the terrace outside the western curtain wall, with attached latrine tower that might be slightly later in date. You can go up the wooden steps to explore further, remembering to look for the garderobe chutes. As you climb, look out through the windows towards Loch Sween and imagine what these waters might have been like full of colourful galleys filled with men at arms.

Castle Sween didn't always stay in the hands of the MacSweens. They were replaced by the Stewart Earls of Menteith during the second half of the 13th century as the Lords of Knapdale. At the beginning of the 14th century the MacSweens attempted to regain the castle. They were supported in this endeavour by Edward II, who wanted to oust the Menteiths as they had rebelled against the crown. The MacSweens found an armed force in residence, so their attempt failed, and the castle remained part of the Menteiths' holdings for another century or more. By the 15th century, Castle Sween was in the possession of the MacDonald Lords of the Isles. The Lords installed a constable, or keeper, and one of these was, of course, Alexander MacMillan.

From the late 15th century, the keepers of the castle were the Campbell Earls of Argyll, to whom it was granted in 1481. They appear to have made few modifications to its fabric. The castle was garrisoned in the 1640s and used as a base to distribute grain imported from Ireland. It is thought to have been captured and burned by Royalist forces in 1647 and then fell into ruin. It continued to be used in part however, as excavations revealed kilns in use after this time.

Head back outside and walk around to the northern wall of the castle. Here you can see the bottom of one of the garderobe chutes.

Look out to sea to spot the boat landing. Castle Sween might have been a good landing spot for thousands of years for boats travelling from Ireland, for two Neolithic stone axes made of a stone that can only be found in Northern Ireland were discovered on the shore here.

Retrace your steps through the caravan park to the road.

Inside Castle Sween

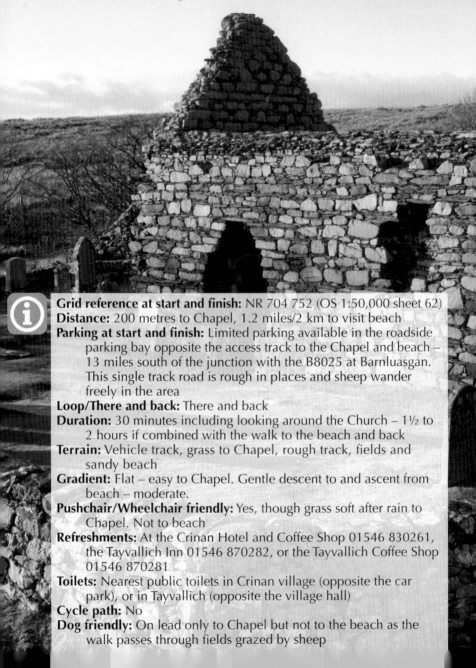

25 KILMORY CHAPEL, KILMORY KNAP AND KILMORY BAY

Medieval crosses and grave slabs and the area's best white sand beach

Grid reference at start and finish: NR 704 752 (OS 1:50,000 sheet 62)

Distance: 200 metres to Chapel, 1.2 miles/2 km to visit beach

Parking at start and finish: Limited parking available in the roadside parking bay opposite the access track to the Chapel and beach – 13 miles south of the junction with the B8025 at Barnluasgan. This single track road is rough in places and sheep wander freely in the area

Loop/There and back: There and back

Duration: 30 minutes including looking around the Church – 1½ to 2 hours if combined with the walk to the beach and back

Terrain: Vehicle track, grass to Chapel, rough track, fields and sandy beach

Gradient: Flat – easy to Chapel. Gentle descent to and ascent from beach – moderate.

Pushchair/Wheelchair friendly: Yes, though grass soft after rain to Chapel. Not to beach

Refreshments: At the Crinan Hotel and Coffee Shop 01546 830261, the Tayvallich Inn 01546 870282, or the Tayvallich Coffee Shop 01546 870281

Toilets: Nearest public toilets in Crinan village (opposite the car park), or in Tayvallich (opposite the village hall)

Cycle path: No

Dog friendly: On lead only to Chapel but not to the beach as the walk passes through fields grazed by sheep

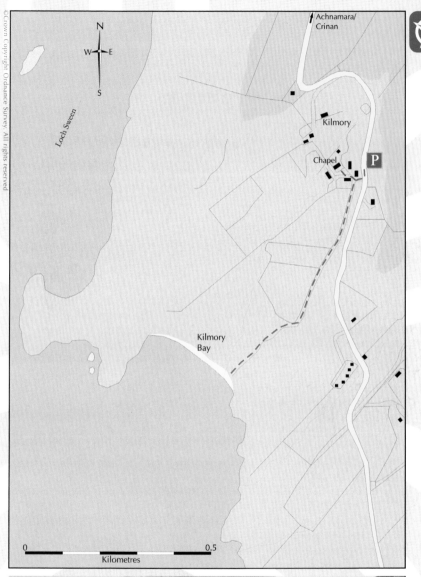

Achnamara/
Crinan

Kilmory

Chapel

P

Loch Sween

Kilmory
Bay

0 — 0.5

Kilometres

The coastline near Kilmory Bay

Walk down the track between stone-built houses then bear right across the grass to the metal gate in the substantial stone wall. The chapel is located in the centre of the township of Kilmory. The houses were originally thatched, and fell into disuse, but have since been restored and extended and are inhabited once again.

The wall around the burial ground is thought to date to the 19th century but there is no evidence of an earlier enclosure sometimes found around very old ecclesiastical sites.

The chapel itself dates to the 13th century, but the possibility that this was not the first ecclesiastical building on the site is demonstrated by the 'Kil' element in the place name. The chapel is thought to have gone out of use during the 16th century, after which it was used as a burial enclosure. It was never a Parish Church, rather a dependency of Keills, which is located on the peninsula you can see jutting into Loch Swein opposite (walk 23). Kilmory Chapel is thought to be dedicated to Mary but local tradition suggests that the association is in fact with St Maelrubha, who founded a monastery at Applecross in the 7th century AD.

Many sites are associated with this Irish monk for he had previously travelled extensively in Argyll before moving north.

Just before you enter, note the quern stone and rock cut stone on the left of the doorway. These were found in the graveyard – the quern may have been used as a grave marker.

Use the large old key and latch to open the door into the chapel. The walls survive almost to their full height, but the roof is a 1930s addition, built to protect the stones you will see inside. Only one stone (24) has been brought from elsewhere, the rest were either already in the chapel, or were brought in from the graveyard. Look out for the remnants of plaster on the inside of the south and east walls. All the interior walls would once have been plastered. Note also the round headed windows, one of which has been blocked up. Many of the original dressed stones from around the windows have been removed. Look out for the aumbry in the eastern wall, near where the altar would have stood. This recess or cupboard was used to store chalices and other objects used in services.

There are carved grave slabs and crosses displayed around the walls of this chapel.

The earliest stones are crosses which date to the early Christian period. They are arranged around the wall to your left as you enter.

Many of the other stones are medieval grave markers and, as you will see, they are carved with a variety of motifs including shears, swords, helmeted warriors, clergy and fantastical beasts. This kind of carved stone is peculiar to the West Highlands in the medieval period and was popular for around 400 years. Many styles influenced the carvers, including Celtic, Norse and Romanesque models, but many motifs are very peculiar to this area.

Look out for the birlinns (sailing galleys) - these are quite rare, but the fact that there are three stones of this kind at Kilmory speaks perhaps of the strategic importance of birlinns in moving men and arms around the coast. They all date to the 15th century, when the Lordship of the Isles was the dominant force in the area. Look out also for the otter chasing a salmon. Animals often make an appearance in the carvings. Note too, the styles of clothing on some of the figures – all men - reflecting perhaps their comparatively high social status during this time.

The cross towards the altar end of the Church is the best known, and perhaps most accomplished, of all the carvings. It is MacMillan's Cross, which once stood in the graveyard outside. This wonderfully carved and well

preserved disc headed cross was erected by Alexander MacMillan, keeper of Castle Sween for the Lord of the Isles in the 1470s. Look out for the hunting scene with the woodsman looking on, and see if you can spot the faint remains of a possible sundial scratched on the base.

MacMillan's Cross

More information about the carved stones can be found in the Chapel.

Researchers have divided the stones into three schools or styles of carving – these being the Iona, Kintyre and Loch Awe Schools. Some of the stones here are thought to be products of the Iona School, but we can be fairly certain that the stone used was quarried nearby. This might indicate that carvers travelled, and so the groupings relating to stone type and carving style are a reflection of where the stones ended up, rather than were they started.

A visit to the Chapel can easily be extended by a walk to the beautiful beach at Kilmory Knap – see below for directions.

Kilmory Bay Beach

A few metres down the chapel access track a rough sign points towards a muddy track to the left – bear left in front of the first house called Comraich. Straightaway there are fine views westwards towards the Isles of Jura and Islay. Continue along the access track until you reach a gate; go through the gate and cross the field until you reach the beach.

The coastal waters off this part of the west coast of Scotland are extraordinarily diverse. You might see gannets diving offshore, or a flock of sandpipers busy hunting tasty morsels to eat. You might even find yourself watched by a curious seal.

Once at the beach we recommend that you turn right and walk along the sand, then across small areas of grass between the rocks to a patch of shingle. Near here you can overlook the narrow strait between the mainland and tiny Eilean a' Chapuill, on

which stands a World War II Nissen hut.

Look out for coastal wildflowers such as sea pink. Otters are known to hunt here, and if you are very quiet, you might be lucky enough to see one.

Retrace your steps along the beach and return along the access track to the car park. As you return look to your left; at the summit of the small hill you will see a triangular cairn. This is known as Dùn Fhuarlit – it is actually a Bronze Age burial

cairn on top of which has been erected a modern marker cairn.

There are other prehistoric monuments in the area, and discoveries of Bronze Age pottery in a burial cist and a flint knife (which can be seen in Kilmartin Museum) show that the area around Kilmory was used in prehistory.

Kilmory Bay beach

Where to find out more

The following is a list of key publications about the archaeology, history and natural history of Kilmartin Glen and the wider area of Argyll to help you find out more about this fascinating place. You can find a full bibliography on our website www.kilmartin.org

ALCOCK, L. 2003. *Kings and Warriors, Craftsmen and Priests in northern Britain AD 550-850*. Edinburgh: Society of Antiquaries of Scotland Monograph.

ARMIT, I. 2005. *Celtic Scotland; Iron Age Scotland in its European Context*. London: Batsford.

ASHMORE, P.J. 1996. *Neolithic and Bronze Age Scotland*. London: Batsford.

BANNERMAN, J. 1974. *Studies in the History of Dalriada*. Edinburgh: Scottish Academic Press.

BARROW, G.W.S. 1973. *The Kingdom of the Scots: Government, Church and Society from the Eleventh to the Fourteenth Century*. London: Edward Arnold.

BECKENSALL, S. 2005. *The Prehistoric Rock Art of Kilmartin*. Kilmartin: Kilmartin House Trust.

BOARDMAN, S.I. 2006. *The Campbells: 1250-1513*. Edinburgh: John Donald.

BRADLEY, R. 1997. *Rock Art and the Prehistory of Atlantic Europe: Signing the Land*. London: Routledge.

BUTTER, R. 1999. *Kilmartin: Scotland's Richest Prehistoric Landscape: an Introduction and Guide*. Kilmartin: Kilmartin House Trust.

CAMPBELL, E. 1999. *Saints and Sea-Kings: the First Kingdom of the Scots*, Edinburgh: Canongate.

CAMPBELL, M. 2001. *Argyll: The Enduring Heartland*. Colonsay: House of Lochar.

CRONE, A., CAMPBELL, E. and BATEY, C.E. 2005. *A Crannog of the First Millennium AD: excavations by Jack Scott at Loch Glashan, Argyll, 1960*. Edinburgh: The Society of Antiquaries of Scotland.

ELPHINSTONE, M. 2009. *The Gathering Night*. Edinburgh: Canongate.

FISHER, I. 2001. *Early Medieval Sculpture in the West Highlands and Islands*. Edinburgh: RCAHMS.

FOSTER, S.M. 1996. *Picts, Gaels and Scots; Early Historic Scotland*. London: Batsford.

FRASER, J.E. 2009. *From Caledonia to Pictland – Scotland to 795*. Edinburgh: Edinburgh University Press.

JONES, A., FREEDMAN, D., O'CONNOR, B., LAMDIN-WHYMARK, H., TIPPING R., and WATSON, A. (eds.) 2011. *An Animate Landscape: Rock Art and the Prehistory of Kilmartin, Argyll, Scotland*. Oxford: Oxbow.

LANE, A. and CAMPBELL, E. 2001. *Dunadd: an Early Dalriadic Capital*. Oxford: Oxbow.

MACDONALD, R.A. 1997. *The Kingdom of the Isles: Scotland's Western Seaboard, c.1100-1336*. East Linton: Tuckwell.

MÁRKUS, G. (transl) 2008. *Adomnáns 'Law of the Innocents':*

Cáin Adomnáin: a seventh century law for the protection of non combatants. Kilmartin: Kilmartin House Trust.

MARSDEN, J. 2000. *Somerled and the Emergence of Gaelic Scotland*. East Linton: Tuckwell.

MCGEACHY, R.A.A. 2005. *Argyll, 1730-1850: Commerce, Community and Culture*. Edinburgh: John Donald.

MITHEN, S.J. 2000. *Hunter-gatherer Landscape Archaeology: The Southern Hebrides Mesolithic Project 1988-1998 Volumes I and II*. Cambridge: McDonald Institute for Archaeological Research.

MITHEN, S.J. 2010. *To the Islands: An Archaeologist's Relentless Quest to Find the Prehistoric Hunter-Gatherers of the Hebrides*. Isle of Lewis: Two Ravens Press.

MORRISON, I.A. 1985. *Landscape with Lake Dwellings: the Crannogs of Scotland*. Edinburgh: Edinburgh University Press.

OMAND, D. (ed.) 2004. *The Argyll Book*. Edinburgh: Birlinn.

POLLARD, T. and MORRISON, A (eds.) 1996. *The Early Prehistory of Scotland*. Edinburgh: Edinburgh University Press.

RCAHMS, 1988. *Argyll: an Inventory of the Monuments: Volume 6: Mid-Argyll and Cowal, Prehistoric and Early Historic Monuments*. Edinburgh: HMSO.

RCAHMS, 1992. *Argyll: an Inventory of the Monuments*. Volume 7: Mid Argyll and Cowal, Medieval and Later Historic Monuments, Edinburgh: HMSO.

RCAHMS, 2008. *Kilmartin: An Inventory of the Monuments extracted from Argyll Volume 6: Prehistoric and Early Historic Monuments*. Edinburgh: HMSO.

RITCHIE, J.N.G. (ed.) 1997. *The Archaeology of Argyll*. Edinburgh: Edinburgh University Press.

SMITH, C. 1992. *Late Stone Age Hunters of the British Isles*. London: Routledge.

SMOUT, T.C. (ed.) 1993. *Scotland since Prehistory: Natural Change and Human Impact*. Aberdeen: Scottish Cultural Press.

SMOUT, T.C. (ed.) 2003. *People and Woods in Scotland: a History*. Edinburgh: Edinburgh University Press.

SMYTH, A.P. 1984. *Warlords and Holy Men: Scotland AD 80-1000*. London: Edward Arnold.

WALKER, F.A. 2000. *The Buildings of Scotland: Argyll and Bute*. London: Penguin.

WICKHAM-JONES, C.R. 1994 *Scotland's First Settlers. London: Batsford*.

WICKHAM-JONES, C.R. 2001. *The Landscape of Scotland*. Stroud: Tempus.

WOOLF, A. 2007. *From Pictland to Alba: 789-1070*. Edinburgh: Edinburgh University Press.

YEOMAN, P. 1995. *Medieval Scotland: an Archaeological Perspective*. Edinburgh: Batsford.